C000172718

Coach Yourself
to Confidence

Single and Loving It

Coach Yourself
to Confidence

WENDY BRISTOW

Thorsons

PUBLISHED IN ASSOCIATION WITH
COSMOPOLITAN

Thorsons
An Imprint of HarperCollins*Publishers*
77–85 Fulham Palace Road,
Hammersmith, London W6 8JB

The Thorsons website address is: www.thorsons.com

Published by Thorsons in association
with *Cosmopolitan* magazine 2001

10 9 8 7 6 5 4 3 2

A catalogue record for this book
is available from the British Library

ISBN 0 00 712009 5

Printed and bound in Great Britain by
Clays Ltd, St Ives plc

Contents

Acknowledgements

Huge thanks to Emma Dally and Carole Tonkinson for having the idea for this book and then making it happen.

I'm grateful to the people at two organizations that have helped me learn more about confidence – Spectrum and Communications Skills Europe – and have contributed some great self-coaching exercises, which really work. Also, all the women who shared their stories with me and the experts who shared their thoughts with me, especially Maggie McKenzie, Bob Griffiths and Sandra Donaldson. And to Barbara Vesey for a great copy-edit.

A special thanks to Jeremy for increasing my confidence and relationships by having one with me where I can truly be myself.

Oh, and thanks to my mother who, as she likes to point out, had me in the first place.

Introduction

What makes *me* qualified to talk to you about confidence?

First and foremost, I would say I'm a confident person, which is a good start. But I haven't always been this way (and, as we'll see, even generally confident people aren't confident all the time). I wasn't born confident. I didn't have the kind of childhood that instills self-assurance at every step. I haven't been to any confidence school; I haven't majored in bravery and courage at some strange university of self-help.

I've had to learn how to be confident myself, dragging myself up by my confident bootstraps.

In my working life, I have edited and launched one magazine (the young women's magazine *More!*, launched in 1988) and worked on the launches of two others, one of which was in Australia. Launching magazines takes confidence. For the past 10 years I have worked as a freelance journalist, writing about psychology and relationships, which, more often than not, comes down to confidence. And I train other writers and journalists in various writing and editing skills and to manage their staff. Which also, more often than not, comes down to confidence.

When people come on my training courses, they fill in a form telling me what they want from the course. I've lost count of the number of times people have said 'I want more confidence.' And always, once they've talked about their jobs, their problems in their jobs and done some practice in the safe arena of the training room, they do go away more confident.

If I could bottle the confidence people get on my courses, I'd make millions. But, of course, confidence doesn't work that way. So I've done the next best thing. I've written a book about it.

In this book is everything you need to coach yourself to become more confident.

It takes confidence to live a fulfilling life. Unless you spend your time quivering under a stone, life tends to throw challenges which require some kind of courage – to speak up for yourself, to say no, to ask for what you want, to leave your job or your lover, to find a new job or a new lover – every day.

The way I've become more confident over the years is by picking up the tools which work and then coaching myself with them.

That is what this book is about. It presents you with the tool kit for building greater self-confidence, and tells you how to encourage yourself, look after yourself, coach yourself forward, as you use them.

The tools in this book are tried and tested and guaranteed to get you through any confidence-wobbling situation. All you have to do is try-and-test them for yourself and coach yourself accordingly. They work for me. They can work for you too. All you have to do is practise, practise, practise. And – hopefully – have fun while you're about it. I hope you do.

Good luck!

Wendy Bristow
Islington, March 2001

1

What's Holding You Back?

1

Hello, Ms Confident – Yes, *You!*

I didn't become more confident overnight. It was a process. And some areas were slower to catch up than others. But there were definite confidence milestones. Like buying my own flat, trusting myself enough to know I could do all that, from choosing a place that wouldn't fall down to negotiating scary amounts of money. Then, when my best friend got ill when we were travelling in Turkey and I had to deal with it and get her home – that made me feel, 'If I can do that, and not even in my own language, I can do anything!'
Amanda, 27

You've picked up this book because you'd like to be more confident. Wouldn't we all? Yes, it's true, even confident people aren't confident all the time. When they're not, they fake it. This book is about how to fake it and, then, how by faking it you'll begin to feel it for real. You can – and will – become your own confidence coach, your own best self-boosting buddy, being there for yourself through all the insecurity-provoking challenges life tends to throw at us.

But first we need to bust a few myths ...

Confidence Myth #1: Some People Are Confident All the Time

This is not true. Even confident-seeming people are unconfident sometimes. Like you, they have some areas they are less confident in than others. I know several women who are positively thrusting in their careers, but faced with an attractive, eligible man, they go wobblier than week-old jelly. I know several brilliant journalists who, when they contemplate writing a novel, suddenly can't believe they could ever string a sentence together worth showing.

Also, whenever we take on a new challenge we have fears we won't be able to do it. It's natural. It's part of being human. Take me, right now. I feel pretty confident I can tackle more or less any kind of journalism, and I've written one book already, but faced with starting a whole new book, *ohmigod*.

If you buy into this particular myth you keep yourself stuck in 'us and them' thinking – 'I'm just not confident so I might as well give up now.' This is not good, and it's not true. So stop it. Now.

In my opinion, people who reckon they never experience crises of confidence are either lying or they've got something seriously wrong somewhere ...

Myth #2: Some People Are Just Born Confident (Like It's a Personality Trait or a Talent)

Again, balderdash. Think of famous people. Many are also famously insecure. They just have a funny way of showing it. Their desire for fame and success outweighs (just) their fear of failure and lack of confidence.

Think about Michelle Pfeiffer who, for much of her early life, was convinced she looked like a duck. It didn't stop her becoming an actress and a sex symbol.

Yes some people have more front, more self-belief, more, if you like, *balls* than others. But front, self-belief and balls are things you can cultivate. (Well, maybe not the balls.)

Myth #3: I Had All My Confidence, All My Self-belief, Knocked Out of Me as a Child and I'll Never Get It Back

If this were true I wouldn't be sitting here writing a book about how to coach yourself to more confidence. I'd be out with some other moaning minnie playing the game of 'ain't it awful'. If you did have a dreadful childhood, if you were bullied at school or had critical parents who didn't believe you were capable of amounting to anything, that's very sad and I'm genuinely sorry. But really and truly your childhood does not have to cast a black cloud over your whole unconfident life. That would only be compounding the problem, making it life-long and lasting.

Yes, people whose parents were genuinely supportive of their child's every caprice and crappy school report do have an easier start on the confidence ladder, but there aren't many of them around. People who had a difficult start in life often use it as a springboard to great achievements. Madonna lost her mother and it made her a megastar. Tracey Ullman's father died when she was five and the comedy skills she honed to put a smile on her bereaved mother's face made her one of the highest-paid women in the world. John Cleese's childhood left him with a well of unresolved anger which he used to fuel his manic millionaire-making

TV rantings in *Monty Python* and *Fawlty Towers*. Elton John didn't get on with his Dad … You get the gist. And where did all their confidence come from? Ultimately, from themselves.

Once we've bust these myths there are no excuses. We can start working that confidence muscle right now. But first, let's be crystal clear about what we're talking about here.

What Confidence Is

I define confidence as a feeling of capability. That I am capable of handling myself in social and work situations and I can really rely on myself. I don't think we necessarily all have this feeling to start with. It's linked to experience.

Maggie McKenzie, Director of the Spectrum Psychotherapy Centre in London

The dictionary definition of confidence, even though it's taken from *The Shorter Oxford English Dictionary*, still goes on a bit. It includes phrases like:

1   the mental attitude of trusting in or relying on;

2   assured expectation;

3   assurance arising from relying (on yourself, circumstances, etc.);

4   feeling certain, fully assured, sure;

5   full of assurance, self-reliant, bold; having no fear of failure.

Confidence, then, is the feeling or sense that, yes, I'm going to do OK in this situation, I can handle it. Fear of failure is its opposite.

What it all boils down to, as Maggie McKenzie says above, is competence and capability. When we know, without question, we can do something, when we don't doubt it for a minute, we're so confident about it we don't even know we are. For example, say I decide to take the rubbish out. I know that I know how to take the rubbish out. I know I walk downstairs (and I've done that millions of times, so I know how to do it). I walk to the bin, lift up the lid. Pull out the black bin bag, tie it at the top, walk out through the hall carrying the bin bag, open the front door and sling it out on the street. Do I have the slightest doubt, the slightest eensy-weensy inkling of anxiety that I might mess up? No. Therefore I am totally confident. I believe in my ability to do it. The technical term for this is 'unconscious competence'.

When we learn to do something we go through four stages:

1   Unconscious incompetence — we don't know we can't do it

2   Conscious incompetence — we do know (only too well) we can't do it

3   Conscious competence — Hoorah! We know we can do it

4   Unconscious competence — we don't even realize we know how to do it.

Until I started thinking about the rubbish just now (and I know it might seem like I'm labouring this, but bear with me), I didn't even know I was confident about putting it out. I had reached unconscious competence.

We go through these four stages with everything we do. Think about when you learned to drive a car. Remember how consciously incompetent you felt when you first started? Then, as you passed your test and for a period afterwards, you were hyper-aware on the road that, though you knew how to do it, it was all new and strange. And now, if you're a regular driver, you'll be able to drive, eat, talk on a mobile phone (naughty) and plan tonight's dinner all at once while some unconscious, automatic part of your brain does the driving. (Although hopefully not too unconscious. Far be it from me to be encouraging reckless driving.)

The four stages tell us some useful things about confidence.

► They explain why everyone feels less confident about things they don't know how to do too well yet; or in unfamiliar situations, or with new challenges (all of which bring up conscious incompetence).
► They demonstrate the intimate relationship between confidence and competence (or capability).

So, in a nutshell, all you have to do is tell yourself you know how to do something and – wayhey – you're off.

Q: But what if what I don't know how to do is be confident?

A: That's what this book is about. By the time you've read it through to the last page, you'll *know* how to be

confident. Then all you'll have do is keep practising
until confidence is a skill that comes as naturally to
you as driving the car or putting the rubbish out …

Cook that Soup – the Confidence Recipe

Confidence is made up one part each of:

- ▶ Competence 'I know I can do it – I've done it before'
- ▶ Capability 'I know I can do it – I have the skills'
- ▶ Self-belief – believing 'I can do it'
- ▶ Self-trust 'I trust myself to do it'
- ▶ Willingness 'I am willing to do it.'

Now we know what we're dealing with, let's get on and do it. But
first, here are some tricks for faking it while you're making it.

Faking It While You're Making It: 21 Ways

Use these confidence tricks for any situations which bring up feelings of 'conscious incompetence'.

1   Smile – It's what confident-feeling people do and it
       prevents your facial muscles crumpling up into
       something that looks like terror, and also stops your
       chin shaking.

2   Stand up straight – Slumpy posture says 'I'm scared,'
       'I'm defeated,' 'I'm giving up.'

3   Make eye contact. Confident people have a direct gaze.

4   Breathe. When we're scared we stop breathing. Result?

We feel more scared. Breathing instantly makes you feel better, sound better.

5   Speak slowly. Nervous people gabble and it's a dead giveaway they're nervous. Speaking slowly sends your brain a message you're in charge.

6   Dress up – high heels, a smart top, whatever makes *you* feel good and in control.

7   Ask for time – you don't have to make all your decisions instantly. No matter whom you're trying to be more confident with, asking for time when someone asks you to do something is a good idea. Then you can formulate a confident reply.

8   Speak up. When we don't feel confident we mutter or speak quietly. Confident people speak up. This can make a difference to how people perceive you.

9   Stand up, period. Stand up to make difficult phone calls, to deal with difficult people.

10 Buy some confident clothes. Red is a good confident colour and wearing it can make you feel better about yourself. It also gives off a subliminal message to others that you mean business.

11 Have a confidence touchstone – an image, a phrase which reminds you you can be confident.

12 Write down a confident phrase and put it in your pocket. You can physically touch it when you need the

reassurance of its message. I did this one tricky time using Eleanor Roosevelt's quote: 'No one can make you feel inferior without your consent.' It worked.

13 Feel your feet on the floor. When we're feeling nervous we often shoot up into our heads, creating that spaced-out sensation. Feeling your feet helps you feel grounded, calmer, confident-er.

14 Imagine you're playing a confident person in a play that has an audience of only one — you. Experiment with this so you can do it in front of someone else. They won't realize.

15 Think about your confident role model and imagine, what would they say in this circumstance? What would they do?

16 Use email — people often find they can sound more confident than they feel in this medium.

17 Use confident affirmations. These are positive statements about yourself and can be very powerful. My friend Sue, newly made a boss, says: 'I go into the building, into the office telling myself "I am a powerful person today" and it really works. You wouldn't recognize me.'

18 Ditto visualization. Before a challenging situation, consciously see yourself in your mind's eye — standing up straight, looking confident, being in control, saying what you want to say. Then remember what you saw when you're in it.

19   Talk to yourself confidently. Whatever you're doing, remind yourself you can do it; remind yourself what your capabilities are. Do not allow yourself to listen to the doubty, creepy voice which tells you this is rubbish and so are you. Talk to yourself like your own best friend.

20   Just before a scary situation, scan your body and find a part that feels relatively OK. It might only be one hand – or your left elbow. Focus all your attention for a moment on that part. Then, when you're in the scary situation, keep bringing your attention back to that part. It will ground you.

21   Try Rescue Remedy – the calming Bach flower remedy available in health food shops and some chemists. Whether you're nervous before a date, an operation or a transatlantic flight, it does the job.

Exercise

I Can, Too, Do Great Things …

Make a list – even if you write it in your head – of things you know you can do. They could be as simple as putting the rubbish out. Just jot down things you're entirely confident you can do.

Make a second list of your major accomplishments in life. List at least five achievements – learning to drive, passing your A levels, getting your first job, getting promoted, recovering from an illness – whatever. The point of this exercise is for you to recognize that, yes, there are things you can do and there are things you've accomplished.

Quiz

Let's find out how confident you are right now. This quiz assesses your confident attitudes.

1   It's important to agree with people in authority, to keep on the right side of them.
Agree A ☐   *Disagree B* ☐

2   Criticism is a terrible thing and obviously destroys the person on the receiving end.
Disagree A ☐   *Agree B* ☐

3   I trust my intuition and often act on it.
Agree A ☐   *Disagree B* ☐

4   Failure is a dreadful and a devastating thing.
Agree A ☐   *Disagree B* ☐

5   Most people I know judge me harshly, as I do them.
Agree A ☐   *Disagree B* ☐

6   If you can't do something well, there's not much point doing it at all.
Agree A ☐   *Disagree B* ☐

7   It's no big deal if not everyone you meet likes you.
Disagree A ☐   *Agree B* ☐

8   People who are confident are more worthy than
        those who are not.
        Agree A ☐   *Disagree B* ☐

9   My successes wouldn't happen without lots of luck as
        well.
        Agree A ☐   *Disagree B* ☐

10   Most people, when they praise me, do it out of a
        need to be polite.
        Agree A ☐   *Disagree B* ☐

11   I love to stand out in a crowd.
        Disagree A ☐   *Agree B* ☐

12   A poor performance signals real future problems.
        Agree A ☐   *Disagree B* ☐

How to Score

Add up your number of As.

10 or more
Congratulations on buying this book, it's just what you need.
This is a very high score, indicating you're carrying around
confidence-denters such as perfectionism and what psychologists
call 'impostor syndrome' – the idea you are a fake and one day
will be found out (for more on this, see page 46). You doubt
yourself and your abilities and overestimate how badly things are
going when you are in charge. But don't worry. We're about to
change all that.

Between 6 and 9
An above-average score. There's still a lot of work to do on the confidence-building front, and you're likely to be living with a high level of anxiety. Some of your beliefs and attitudes are interfering with your ability to trust yourself to tackle tasks which stretch you — which could be anything from asking a man out to stopping yourself saying yes to things you don't really want to do. But you have the potential to live a braver, happier, more confident life. Working with the tools in this book will help you no end.

Between 3 and 6
An average score. Most people could do with improving their general level of confidence, at least in certain anxiety-provoking areas. Most people could benefit from acquiring confidence-boosting skills. Most people would be happier if they weren't so anxious. Once you've mastered the tools in this book, there'll be no stopping you. The world will be yours for the taking.

Between 0 and 3
Lucky you. This is a low score, indicating you've plenty of good, healthy, confidence-building attitudes. Are there some areas where you feel less confident than others? This book will help you build your skills so you can truly tackle anything with confidence.

Now let's see exactly where you're confident and where you're not.

How confident would you feel in the following situations? (without alcohol or any other drug to reduce inhibitions):

Score each of these out of 10 according to how confident you estimate you'd feel that you could pull them off, so that 10 equals 'absolutely confident' and zero equals 'absolutely terrified'.

- ☐ entering a party with a friend
- ☐ entering a party alone
- ☐ asking a man out
- ☐ during sex, asking for an orgasm
- ☐ complaining your meal was cold/overcooked in a restaurant
- ☐ public speaking at work
- ☐ public speaking at a social occasion (e.g. wedding speech)
- ☐ telling a joke with friends
- ☐ job interview
- ☐ calling a company you've always dreamed of working for and asking for work/an interview
- ☐ asking your boss for a raise
- ☐ telling your best friend you are very angry with her
- ☐ taking an exam
- ☐ being seen naked

Any other thoughts about situations in your life where you realize you feel either confident or unconfident? We're all different. Maybe you're very confident at work and in relationships, but the thought of tackling your driving test makes you quiver. Or maybe you're deeply unconfident about your body and physical activities like dancing or making love. Or maybe anything to do with words gives you the heebie-jeebies. The whole point of asking all these nosy questions is to get you shining the spotlight on all those dark corners of lack of confidence so you then have a choice about whether to tackle them or leave them lurking. And it really *is* a choice.

2

Know Your Enemy

Pushing through fear is less frightening than living with the underlying fear that comes from a feeling of helplessness.
Susan Jeffers, *Feel the Fear and Do It Anyway*

In order to fight the good fight on the confidence front, we need to spend some time arming ourselves with information about the weapons in the enemy camp.

Fear

Rosemary tries very hard to be a good manager. She treats her staff well, she cares about them. But one thing she does drives all of them mad – including herself. She lets one – male – subordinate get away with murder. This individual shouts, makes a big noise and generally throws his weight around. Much to Rosemary's and the rest of the staff's annoyance. Why doesn't Rosemary put a stop to it? 'Deep down, I'm frightened of him. I'm scared that if I stand up to him he'll shout louder, and he'll show me up in front of the others. So I do nothing. Deep down I'm not sure how to manage men. I have no doubts about what to do with women, but the thought of tackling Mike simply scares me.'

Fear is the biggie, the #1 enemy underlying any lack of confidence.

Fear is a basic emotion which manifests in a variety of ways: worry, panic, anxiety, defensiveness, boredom, self-doubt, even some anger is merely sitting on top of a big bucket of fear. As in,

'How *dare* he ask me to do that?' (meanwhile inside I'm terrified of tackling it, whatever it is). Or, as in Rosemary's case, it comes out as procrastination.

You watch your boss give a presentation to the whole company and say to yourself, 'I couldn't possibly stand up there and do that.' Why not? Because you're afraid. You see a gorgeous man at the gym and tell yourself 'I'd love to talk with him but I couldn't possibly go over there and start a conversation.' Fear again.

Fear of what? It can take many forms: fear of rejection, fear of making a fool of yourself, fear of 'doing it wrong', of being shown up, fear of failure. The one you choose will be as individual as your taste in pastries.

It's a mistake to think that confident-seeming people don't feel fear. Of course they do. As Susan Jeffers says in the best-known book on the subject, *Feel the Fear and Do It Anyway*, 'Not only are you going to experience fear whenever you're on unfamiliar territory, but so is everyone else!'

How It Harms

It's obvious. Fear damages our confidence by keeping us terrified of taking the risks, making the leaps, tackling the tasks which 'If I were more confident' you would do. Ironically, doing these things is what builds our confidence, as we'll see later.

Criticism

When it comes to criticism, there are two parties involved: them and us.

Them

Jenny wrote a novel which sold for megabucks. One of her so-called friends said 'Oh, you're just lucky.' Thankfully Jenny was confident enough to write the novel in the first place. Imagine if she'd said 'I'm thinking of writing a novel.' What might that Ms Negative have said then?

Criticism is a double-edged sword. Accurate criticism can help you develop your talents and increase your self-awareness. Inaccurate criticism rusts up your confidence and shrivels your self-esteem.

Constant criticism, whether coming from your parents, your partner, so-called friends or your own inner critic can be bad for your health. Leave alone your confidence. Beware people who put you down. Always ask yourself, 'What is their motive for saying this?' It will seldom be good. If someone is criticizing you regularly, you need to stop seeing them regularly.

☆ Star Tip

Always remember criticism is just one person's opinion and may not be accurate or true.

Before paying attention to criticism, ask yourself, was it:

Requested	Not requested
Kind	Unkind
Positive	Negative
Specific	Vague
Fair	Unfair

Pay attention to criticism which falls into the left-hand side of our list. Ignore any which falls into the right-hand side. Pay no attention to people who behave like they know it all. They don't. Especially when it comes to your life. You're the only one who can truly know what's right for you. And criticism is the last vehicle to get you there.

Us

Sometimes our harshest critic is much closer to home. In fact, it lives in our house and eats our cornflakes. All of us, without exception, have an irritating little inner voice that criticizes us, plants doubts and generally badgers us. For some lucky individuals, it just questions: are you sure you're doing this right? Is this what you want?

But for others – probably the majority – it comes in with hobnail boots. 'Who do you think you are? What makes you think you can be any good at this? You're a failure and a failure you'll remain.' Etc., etc.

Psychologists call this part of us various names – 'top dog', the 'inner critic', the 'chatterbox', the 'monkey'. The harshness of its conversation tends to depend on how you were treated as a child. Had a parent who put you down? Your inner voice will do the same. Had a sibling who bullied you? Your inner voice will be a bully too. (If you doubt this, have a listen to your own messages. Do they sound like anyone you know? A parent or sibling, a teacher?)

Constant criticism from your inner voice has the same effect as someone outside doing it. It erodes your confidence, ruins self-esteem. Often the only person holding you back is you. And this voice is the culprit. But – hurrah! – it can be changed. In Part Two we'll show you how.

How It Harms

Just one unfavourable remark can hold us back. Sometimes for a lifetime. Criticism in our childhood can cause us to form negative beliefs about ourselves: 'I'm no good, I'll never amount to anything, my sister's prettier therefore I'm ugly.' Criticism later on can stifle our dreams, cancelling our tiny attempts at breaking out of an unconfident rut.

⚂ Don't Take It Personally

While we're on the subject, make this your mantra: 'I don't take things personally.' Sometimes when we're feeling un-self-confident, we take things that weren't even meant that way as criticism. You're walking along the road and the roadsweeper moans out loud about the 'pigs' who drop litter all over the street. *Does he mean me?* He must mean me. I dropped a Twix wrapper in 1982 and I *think* I threw a banana skin out the car window three months ago.

See how ridiculous this is? Get over it.

Even criticism aimed at *you* needn't be taken personally. Some of it says more about the person who dealt it rather than felt it. Oprah Winfrey says: 'For me, "Don't take anything personally" was life-changing. I took other people's opinions about me to heart. I'd read the tabloids and think, "Why do they say things that aren't true?" And I'd be hurt. [Now I know] everyone's acting out of their own preconceptions. They're in their own personal movie. Knowing that has freed me.'

Perfectionism

Perfectionism is the enemy of confidence because when your personal standards are so high that nothing's ever quite good enough, you never get to feel sure you'll do anything well. Plus you'll never be pleased you *have* done something well, which is the impetus you need for future challenges.

Believe me, I know. I think of myself these days as a 'recovering perfectionist'. I used to be ultra-hard on myself about just about everything – I was never thin enough, my work was never good enough, meals I cooked were never tasty enough … and when I did do things well I picked holes in them. A woman I met on a management course once said to me: 'You're not a perfectionist, you're an impossibilist. You want it right first time.' Fair point.

I now call myself a 'recovering perfectionist' (or impossibilist) because, like a 'recovering alcoholic' I will always feel a lure for the demon – *think*, not drink. But I've kicked the habit and learned to live with the constant temptation to critique myself from here to eternity. And, phew, *what* a relief.

Now I know I can do my best – without expecting perfection (first time). And what I know is, most of the time I do just fine. That, now, is good enough.

How It Harms

Read those first two sentences again.

Victim Thinking

Rachel has never really had a relationship. She's dated lots of people, 'but I hardly ever get past the second drink. Or the second bonk.' Now, at 34, she feels desperate and says 'I just can't do relationships. Other people can do them, not me. So now if a guy seems interested, I just can't be bothered to go through the rigmarole. There's no point. But then I get depressed and think, "When, when will it be my turn?"'

This is a very painful place for Rachel to get to. And it's not made any better by victim thinking, which tends to run along lines of: 'Poor me, I'll never get anywhere. The world is against me.' Rachel is tending this way.

'This might be all right for other people but it'll never work for me.'

'I'm too stupid/depressed/stuck to ever change.'

'My boss gets on at me and erodes my confidence every day.'

'My dad is a bully and knocks the stuffing out of me every time I try to do for myself.'

'So what's the point?'

This, folks, is victim thinking. It has two aspects:

I   feeling sorry for yourself and making excuses for staying stuck

2   blaming other people for the mess you're in; or using
           other people as your excuse for staying stuck, as in 'It's
           his fault. If it weren't for him I'd be doing … blah blah.'

Are you stuck in victim?

Here are some of the classic characteristics of 'poor me' thinking
and behaviours:

▶   moaning a lot, but when people try to offer
           suggestions you get cross and/or defensive
▶   complaining but never taking action
▶   asking for advice but not taking it
▶   playing the game of 'yes, but', as in 'Yes, I know I need
           to do such and such but I can't because …'
▶   using the words 'I can't' a lot when in fact you mean 'I
           won't' or 'I'm choosing not to'
▶   never expressing your anger to people although you
           may *feel* angry a lot of the time
▶   apologizing too often and obsessing about what
           people think of you
▶   putting other people on a pedestal – only to knock
           them off when they do something you don't like.

If you recognize yourself in here (and don't worry if you do, most
of us have some aspect of this going on – and you don't
actually have to *tell* anyone, right?) don't judge yourself. Just use
the awareness that this is a pattern as a first step to change.

How It Harms

Being stuck in victim is a very painful place to be and does *nada*
for your confidence. The thoughts that go with this stance: 'Poor

me, I'll never manage that/Other people can be successful/confident but I can't/ I just can't do that' keep you locked in an 'I can't' mentality when, in fact, you can. Anyone can.

☆ **Star Tip**

It's important to recognize the victim thing is just a habit. It's a conditioned response. You've learned it, at some point, as a way of being in the world. But like any habit it can be changed. And the first step, as with all the nasties in this chapter, is recognition.

Stress

Angelina works in advertising and is usually very confident and competent in her job. But a year ago she took on a challenge that felt too much for her and her confidence plummetted. She says: 'There was so much to do, I felt I didn't have the time to do anything properly. People were always shouting and screaming for this and that – everyone seemed to be dashing around like headless chickens all the time – and the boss was really demanding. I never had a second to myself and while I usually think of myself as a confident person I just went to pieces. I wasn't sure I could do anything anymore.'

When we're stressed we don't give ourselves enough time. How many times have you thought something like, 'Oh *why* did I say I'd do so-and-so? If I'd only stopped to think . . .' But when stressed we never stop to think. We keep going on auto-pilot until we topple over. Or get flu. Or some other stress-related stopping mechanism.

Also, when we're so stressed we don't think straight we don't remember to think confidently. So looking after your stress levels is something you really need to do if you want to coach yourself towards greater confidence.

Facials, massages, exercise, peaceful evenings in alone, talking problems through with friends – these are all stress-releasing pass-times you need to factor in to your everyday life. Knowing you are looking after yourself is a wonderful confidence-booster in itself. It's you demonstrating to yourself – and the world – that you matter.

How It Harms

As I've said, when stressed we tend to revert to old patterns of thinking and doing things, the old and familiar. We haven't the mental or emotional energy to do anything differently. Lack of confidence in itself is a stressor (or, at least, the thoughts and behaviours associated with lack of confidence). In order to change your thoughts and behaviour along more confident lines you don't need to be imitating a hamster in its wheel. It won't happen.

Exercise

Know *Your* Enemy

Now you've read over this chapter, ask yourself, what is standing in the way of you being more confident?

> Perfectionism?
> Stress?
> Your inner critic?
> Someone else's criticism? (or imagined criticism?)
> Victim thinking?

Fear?

All of the above?

Just spend a minute or two pondering:

1   What is it prevents *me* from becoming more
     confident?

2   What are the payoffs of staying stuck with this? What
     do I, secretly, get out of it?

     (These could be, in some way, positive or useful to you,
     e.g. 'I don't have to make any effort'; 'I don't have to
     leave my critical boyfriend and deal with all the hoo-hah
     that would cause'; 'I don't have to face my fear' – or they
     could be negative, e.g. 'I don't have any fun'; 'I'm afraid all
     the time and let fear rule my life'). It's likely there will be
     both positive and negative payoffs/repercussions on
     your list.

Now spend a minute or two pondering:

3   What would be the payoffs of becoming more
     confident?

     For example, 'I might actually *get* that pay rise if I
     summoned up the confidence to ask for it.'

     'I might feel happier and meet someone better suited to
     me if I left my boyfriend.'

'I might get to enjoy sex if I ask for what I want.'

'I might discover I enjoy making presentations.'

'I'd get a degree if I left this job and went to university. Then I'd be qualified.'

'I might feel less stressed all the time if I feel more confident.'

Again, the point of this exercise is NOT to create a list of all that's wrong with you so your inner critic can have a field day, but to increase your awareness.

☆ Star Tip
Awareness is the first step towards change.

3

Faulty Beliefs that Increase Stress (and Decrease Confidence)

Knowing it was my beliefs that were holding me back was a real eye-opener. When these things are pointed out to you, you say My God! How silly! But until then you just run around trying to live up to them.
Sam, 27

When I'm running a course in people management, I always hand a list of these faulty beliefs out early on. I find there's not much point coaching people in the finer points of, say, assertive communication, if they have these beliefs lurking unquestioned somewhere in their consciousness. When they see the list, generally a chuckle of recognition goes around the room, followed by a collective sigh of relief, a delighted 'oh, right' at the recognition that, yes, these things *are* faulty. Many of us carry them around in our heads without ever questioning them.

Have a read and ask yourself which ones are your particular favourites. Mine, historically, has been number seven (I was a perfectionist, remember?). I have driven myself mad for hours on end wondering what the perfect, right thing to do would be in various — too, too numerous — situations. Now I know there is never a 'perfect' solution — just the one I think is right for me right now, or the one I'm going to try, having considered the options.

Many, many people drive themselves mad trying to live out number one. But attempting to please all of the people, all of the time is a set-up for exhaustion and burn-out. And, while you're running round trying to please everyone, who's pleasing you?

Number three is the favourite of those obsessed with control, while number four is the one which illustrates victim thinking.

You can add your own special, individual favourites at the end.

1   I must be loved by everyone and everyone must approve of everything I do.

2   I must be thoroughly competent, adequate and intelligent in all possible respects.

3   It is a terrible catastrophe when things are not as I would like them to be.

4   Unhappiness is the result of external events which are forced on me that I have no control over.

5   It is easier to avoid difficulties and responsibilities in life than to face them.

6   Because something greatly influenced me in the past, it must dictate my current behaviour.

7   There is one perfect solution to every problem, and if it is not found, the result will be terrible.

8   What other people do is vitally important to me and
     I should make every effort to change them to the way
     I think they should be.

9   A person has virtually no control over his or her
     emotions; s/he is their victim and cannot help how
     s/he feels.

10   I must always be right and never make a mistake.

11   _____

12   _____

13   _____

In my training of editors, for example, I often find people have
faulty beliefs they dream up just for their job, like 'as a boss I must
always be in control' or 'as a boss I must have all the answers, all
the time.'

☆ Star Tip

Believing in these faulty ideas is a set-up. They set us up for
perfectionism, they set us up for never feeling confident in
our own abilities, but most of all they set us up for stress. And
stress, as we've already seen, is an enemy of self-confidence.

Stress-busting Beliefs

These are the magic antidotes to the stress-increasing statements
above.

1   I have the right to ask for what I want (realizing the other person has the right to say 'No').

2   I have the right to have opinions, feelings and emotions, and to express them appropriately.

3   I have the right to make statements which have no logical basis and which I don't have to justify (e.g. intuitive ideas and comments).

4   I have the right to make my own decisions and to cope with the consequences.

5   I have the right to choose whether or not to get involved in someone else's problems.

6   I have the right not to know about something and not to understand.

7   I have the right to make mistakes.

8   I have the right to be successful.

9   I have the right to change my mind.

10   I have the right to privacy.

11   I have the right to be alone and independent.

12   I have the right to change myself and to act differently/confidently.

Exercise

Think about which faulty beliefs you've been living by, then find the magic antidote in the second list above which will replace your faulty choices. Use it as an *affirmation*. An affirmation is a positive statement which, when repeated over and over, sinks in and replaces an old negative belief. Choose your new belief (or beliefs) and write them down somewhere where you'll see them; write them a few times every day, stick them in the top of your briefcase, bottom of your rucksack, side of your handbag, on your computer, the toilet door – wherever you'll see them regularly. Repeat them over and over in your head when you're walking to the bus-stop. Whatever you do, repeat them and soon you'll be believing them.

Not-always-obvious Symptoms of Lack of Confidence

Physical

> blushing, rashes, sweating, feeling hot
> slumping, head down, doe-eyed (early Princess Diana)
> breathing quickly and shallowly (which we do when afraid)
> getting ill just before a hot date/exam
> hovering on the outside at parties, gatherings

Emotional

> envy, jealousy
> shyness
> fear/terror
> panic attacks

anger at demands (especially if they demand you be
more confident – *'I can't do that!'*)

Intellectual

thoughts which begin 'I can't,' 'What if?' 'What's the point?'
mental confusion, not being able to think straight
(because fear is underneath)
indecisiveness – lacking the confidence to make a
decision
negative self-talk: 'I'm so stupid,' 'I'm too stupid'
'if only'
comparing – she's better/prettier/slimmer than me
defensiveness

Behavioural

procrastination (i.e. putting things off)
self-justification/defensiveness
criticism/slagging off (usually other people who are
doing things you don't feel confident enough to
tackle)
being late
apologizing
saying yes when you feel no
doing things you don't really want to, because you feel
you have to/have no choice
breaking promises – usually because didn't have the
confidence to say no in the first place
dating people who are less attractive/intelligent/fun
than you are
staying in a bad relationship
letting friends walk all over you

sticking in a job you hate
being nice when you don't feel nice
giving in

Confidence Wobblers

Things that Go Boo! – Knowing What Knocks You Off Your Confident Perch

One minute you're oozing self-belief, feeling like you could take on Tyson in a fight then slope off and pull Brad Pitt, Jennifer or no Jennifer. Next minute you're wobbly as a jelly in a hailstorm. *What happened?*

You spend all day kicking ass in the workplace, then slope off home to cry into your soup about how you can't find a man. *What's going on?*

Sometimes no matter how much we encourage ourselves, how much we think positive and so on, we crumple at certain points. Assertiveness trainers recognize this tendency, and call those triggers our 'crumple buttons'.

The things that crumple us affect our self-confidence. For me, whenever anyone suggests I might have done something wrong, or been 'unreasonable', or 'unfair' or 'hurting on purpose' I tend to over-react. I must value being right and being reasonable, I suppose. Also I was brought up to be 'nice' and, much as I may kick against it, that conditioning is still there and goes into over-drive unless I consciously challenge it. So if anyone suggests I might not be being nice in some way, even though consciously, logically, I think it doesn't matter, emotionally I crumple. Crumpling equals reacting. Whenever we crumple we go into an emotional reaction and we lose it.

These crumple buttons take some excavating, but regard yourself as an archaeologist, fascinated by what you might dig up in these interesting layers that are you. Maybe certain situations wobble you. Maybe what that person just said taps into:

- ▶ a *doubt*, e.g. 'Yes, he's right, I don't know what I'm doing'; 'That's true, I don't know what will happen'; 'It could all go wrong'; 'Maybe I don't have the right to be paid more ...'
- ▶ A *negative belief* you have about yourself, e.g. 'I'm no good with men'; 'I'm boring, I'm not entertaining'; 'I'm not clever'; 'I'll never be a success'; 'Of course no one like me.'
- ▶ A *core belief* you have about yourself which you feel you must maintain or you'll fall apart, for example, 'I'm a nice person, I'm not nasty, it's not good to be nasty, if I'm nasty the world might end.'

Core beliefs are not necessarily the same as the 'faulty beliefs that increase stress' mentioned earlier (although they may be).

Core beliefs affect our beliefs in our competence in certain situations. Core beliefs are not necessarily conscious. You often only realize afterwards that what happened was that a core belief was touched and challenged. (We'll look at these more in the next chapter.)

Another Confidence Wobbler: The 'If It Were Me' Trap

'If it were me ...

> … I wouldn't want to talk to a room full of people, so
> I can't ask that shy person to present.'
> … I wouldn't want to work late.'
> … I wouldn't want to give up my weekend day to
> judge a dog show, so I can't ask this celebrity to.'
> … I would hate being told off by my boss, so I'll be
> really easy on them, even though they've behaved
> appallingly.'

And so on and so on. Often we feel unconfident about making requests or telling the truth because we're worried about the effect on the other person *from our own perspective*.

Point one: Making assumptions about other people is a Bad Idea (as the saying goes: 'assume' makes an 'ass' of 'u' and 'me'). Other people are other people. It's more than likely they'll have different responses to you. Different values, different desires, different emotions. So you can't predict them. That shy person might secretly be desperate to present the team's achievements. That celebrity might adore dogs. That colleague might be a budding workaholic who relishes the chance to stay at their desk beyond dusk. That out-of-order subordinate may secretly desire to be reined in. The only way you'll find out is to put it out there and see.

Point two: You can't rescue people. They can look after themselves. Even if what you ask puts them out, even if they say yes and mean no, THAT'S NOT YOUR PROBLEM.

Bite the bullet and do it anyway, and see what happens.

☆ Star Tip
99 per cent of what we fear will happen never comes true.

Meeting Your Scared Self

Here's another way of looking at confidence wobblers, which comes from the psychotherapeutic school of psychosynthesis. This may or may not work for you, but many people find they can have fun with it, and discover more about themselves in the process.

Psychosynthesis experts regard our personality as made up of a collection of sub-personalities or 'parts' which work independently and sometimes against one another. We dip in and out of the various parts according to the situation, our mood, our goals and how we're provoked.

It explains why we sometimes find ourselves acting 'not ourselves', not how we'd planned, or 'out of character'.

It might be that you have a 'Right, let's do it' part which plans things out, then when you're actually *with* that gorgeous hunk on a date 'little Miss Scaredy Pants' takes over and you're suddenly a quivering wreck.

It can be fun to think about and play around with the idea of sub-personalities. Do you have a scared sub-personality? A part that is a panicker? A Little Miss 'I can't'? The trouble with sub-personalities is that, unrecognized, they can take over.

Just so's you get the idea, here are a couple of mine:

'Mary All-too-much' is a little girl who just wants to sit in the corner with her knees tucked under her chin hoping no one will notice her and hoping 'all this' (challenges, demands, responsibility, whatever) will go away in a minute. Mary is full of fear, scared of

just about everything – writing books, speaking in public, negotiating more money, taking on new training challenges.

And yet I routinely do all these things, so she can't be all of who
I am, right?

Meanwhile, 'Control freak' bosses all the other parts, duffing them
up if their performance isn't up to Control freak's sky-high
standards. This part has no other emotions except anger and
disgruntledness (if you can call that an emotion). There's no room
in his (somehow I feel this part is masculine) repertoire for finer
feelings like fear or shyness. He hardly ever gets excited, either.
He's stuck in a kind of grim march-forward mode.

Now, when I realize one of these parts has come foremost, I can
have an inner talk with myself – ask myself if I'm being too
control-freaky, or if Mary-all-too-much is having a panic. I can
remember that these parts of who I am are not *all* of who I am.

Exercise

Do you have a scared self? What is s/he like? How old? Does s/he
have a name? Could you draw him or her?

What other parts do you have, and can you give them names?
How do they interact? Do they conflict with one another? In
what ways?

Exercise

What would I do if I were truly, truly confident – if fear and lack of confidence weren't an issue?

Don't take too long pondering this. Just write down whatever first comes into your mind.

Tricks Others Use to Bamboozle Us: Identifying Insecurity Triggers

Here you can get really specific about which people, situations and places make you quake – and why.

The Self-assessment Confidence Grid

This grid helps you get clear exactly where your confidence crumple-buttons are. Given that our confidence often reveals itself with others, that's what this grid shows you.

	Work (college)	Friends	Family	Partner	Boss	Colleagues
Expressing positive feelings						
Giving compliments						
Receiving compliments						
Making requests						
Initiating and maintaining conversation						
Refusing requests						
Standing up for your rights						
Refusing invitations						
Expressing personal opinions						
Disagreeing						
Expressing anger constructively						
Criticizing						
Accepting constructive criticism						
Dealing with being verbally attacked						
Saying 'No'						

4

Confidence and Self-esteem

I used to lack confidence because I used to lack self-esteem. I really didn't like myself much at all. Once I started to like myself all sorts of things happened – I finally lost weight, I asked my boss for a rise and got it, I joined a dating agency and met lots of nice people. And all these things helped me get much more confidence. I think it's hard to think about my confidence without thinking about my self-esteem, which used to be rock-bottom and is now, really, quite good and getting better all the time.
Hannah, 35

Like Hannah says, there is an intimate link between confidence and self-esteem. It's impossible to feel confident if you live with a chronic sense of 'I'm not good enough,' which is what low self-esteem is.

Symptoms of low self-esteem and lack of confidence are remarkably similar:

> not believing in yourself
> thinking others are better than you
> putting yourself down
> feeling/thinking like a victim
> feelings of failure
> feelings/beliefs of 'I'm no good/not good enough'
> indecision
> fearfulness
> fear of taking risks

poor communication skills – apologizing, prevaricating, saying yes when you mean no
letting other people take advantage of you …

… and so on.

Low self-esteem is so tragically common as to seem part of the human condition. I know when I'm training or coaching and people hit problem spots, there's usually some self-esteem beastie lurking underneath. They don't feel they have the right to tell their staff what to do; or they criticize their work so mercilessly they never get to enjoy it or, indeed, go home on time. Low self-esteem reveals itself in all sorts of insidious ways and holds people back in all sorts of unnecessary and tragic fashions.

Many, many people suffer low self-esteem in one area – the most common ones being appearance, work and relationships. There may be a few lucky individuals on this earth who totally believe in themselves. Like Dawn French, who grew up with her parents telling her she was beautiful and she could do anything. But most of us have some degree of feeling bad. Women are especially good at feeling bad about themselves. We're not pretty enough or talented enough or rich enough or funny enough or, indeed, confident enough.

Amy is gorgeous and funny. She has a great job, but she can't seem to find a relationship.

Rowena is top-notch intelligent and a brilliant organizer, but just doesn't see herself as 'a career woman' so stays stuck in a dead-end job which doesn't suit her personality and where her boss behaves obnoxiously.

Christine goes out with any man who asks her, then spends her time obsessing why the relationship didn't work – again.

Joanna is perfectly attractive but is convinced deep down she's ugly. This has manifested as an obsession with her weight, which has now sadly developed into an eating disorder. Which only makes her feel worse about herself.

Lorna has a high-powered job – so high-powered there's always an enormous amount to do. And Lorna just can't say no, so she ends up working all hours and her relationship has begun to suffer. Unable to say no or set limits with either partner or boss, Lorna is wearing herself into a stressed-out unconfident frazzle as she tries to please everyone except herself.

Julie is always the life and soul of the party. She has a good job with a record company and is the most popular executive with all the bands. She flirts like mad, but when any tasty males ask her out, Julie makes some excuse. She says 'I've realized I'm terrified of a relationship. If someone really got to know me they'd find out I'm not someone you'd would want to spend time with.' All her friends think this is nuts, but Julie really believes it.

If the low self-esteem we're talking about belongs to you, we need to tackle it as part of your confidence-building programme.

Cracking Core Beliefs

Whether we're looking at lack of confidence or lack of self-esteem, the core problem is the same: core beliefs.

It might be that your first love dumped you and you decided there and then you weren't lovable. It might be that the kids at school picked on you – for your weight, your clothes, your nose – and you decided your appearance was unacceptable. It might be your parents had impossible standards you could never live up to and you decided nothing you could ever do would be good enough. These are where these beliefs come from. We decide, at some point, that we're bad, unlovable, whatever, and our self-esteem takes a knock-out punch.

The belief we're somehow not good enough then becomes part of who we are – unquestioned like our preference for white chocolate over dark or the 'fact' we're crap at maths. It becomes part of our identity. A part of our identity which doesn't really serve us. And, fortunately, a part which can be changed.

Negative beliefs lurk behind both lack of confidence and low self-esteem:

> I don't believe in myself.
> I'm no good.
> I'm a failure.
> I'll never be a success.
> Success is for other people, not for me.
> I'm ugly/too fat/unattractive.
> I'm deep-down bad.
> I'm unlovable – no one will ever love me.

Exercise

Core Beliefs

Take a moment to list beliefs you hold about yourself, good and bad. Write down ones you've read here and identify with, and any others of your own that pop into your head.

Write them in a left hand column, then fill in the other two columns as in this example:

I am ...	Where did I learn this?	Is it true?
Nice	My mother	Not always!
Small	Life	Physically it's true but this doesn't mean I'm insignificant
_____	_____	_____
_____	_____	_____

Are You an Impostor?

Even people who function in a confident-seeming way in the world can have these beliefs lurking around. They feel fakes and suspect that one day they'll be found out and exposed for the fakes they are. This is so common psychologists have a name for it: 'impostor syndrome'. To find out whether you are vulnerable to it, try this test.

Who? Little Old Me? The Impostor Syndrome Test

Answer these questions with: Almost never, Sometimes, Often, Almost always

1   In some situations I feel like a fraud, like I'm not as genuine as others think I am.

2   I feel there's something false or misleading about me that others don't notice.

3   I would describe myself as an 'authentic person'.

4   I generalize negative feelings about myself which stem from a specific incident or situation to other, sometimes unrelated situations.

5   My true self is something that I keep secret and share with very few people.

6   I don't know who I really am and what I really want.

7   If I get a great deal of praise and recognition for something I've accomplished, I belittle the significance of what I've done to myself and others.

8   When people praise me for something I've achieved, I have no doubt that I will be able to live up to their expectations of me in the future.

Scoring

For statements 1, 2, 4—8, for every 'Almost never' give yourself a 1.
Sometimes = 2
Often = 3
Almost always = 4
For statements 3 and 8, Almost always = 1; Often = 2; Sometimes = 3; Almost never = 4

The higher your score, the greater your symptoms of Impostor Syndrome. If your score is 21 or greater, this is a problem for you that you really need to address.

So What Can You Do?

Scratch a successful person and you often find a sufferer of Impostor Syndrome lurking underneath. Like Rachel, 30, a successful account handler at a design agency, who says: 'I started here as a secretary and I'm sure I only got the job because of my looks. Then I have a suspicion I only got promoted because the director fancies me. I can't stop worrying. I know it's stupid but, deep down, my looks are all I feel I have.' Even so, knowing she looks good gives her no satisfaction. 'I feel furious with my friends and colleagues because they all envy and look up to me. Can't they see I hate who I am? – A shallow person whose only accomplishment in life is to look good.'

Women are more likely than men to be prey to Impostor Syndrome. Kay Deaux, a researcher at New York University, found that by age 10 girls are filled with self-doubt and discounting high achievements. Deaux found girls and women are far more likely than men to attribute successes to temporary causes like luck or great effort. Men and boys are more likely to attribute successes to ability. But when they hit up against failure, the sexes work the other way around: women are more likely to attribute it to lack of ability while men blame bad luck or the difficulty of the task.

All this keeps us trapped in a world where talent and success are transitory illusions and failure and exposure lurk forever just round the corner.

As if it wasn't bad enough living with a sense of inauthenticity and self-doubt, sufferers from Impostor Syndrome also live with high levels of anxiety (will I be found out? Can I *really* carry this off?). They also feel vulnerable to exposure and are constantly defending themselves against it. All this eats up huge amounts of energy. Maintaining a false self – who appears confident and capable, while your real self cowers in the corner – puts you under chronic and intense stress. And we've already seen how stress compounds any confidence problems. That's why it's important to work on your core beliefs. It's OK to fake confidence while you're building it, but faking it forever without building a bedrock takes a huge toll.

Impostor Syndrome is just another aspect of low self-esteem; just another way negative beliefs about yourself are showing up.

How Negative Beliefs Become Self-fulfilling Prophecies

Research into confidence, and the lack of it, revealed the phenomenon of the **self-fulfilling prophecy**. These prophecies spin directly out of our beliefs and reveal how our beliefs impact the world.

An example of a positive self-fulfilling prophecy would be if you believe, 'Lori will probably like me if I talk with her.' That belief alone could cause you to start a conversation with Lori and be friendlier to her. Thus, the *belief alone actually increased the probability that it would be fulfilled* (since the *belief* actually helped cause the *action* that helped cause the *prophecy's fulfilment*.)

But it works both ways.

A negative self-fulfilling prophecy would be your belief, 'Lori will probably *not* like me if I talk with her.' That belief would probably prevent you from speaking to Lori or cause you to be less friendly to her. In turn, Lori may not like you because you aren't friendly to her.

Fortunately, all the thoughts and exercises in this book will help boost low self-esteem and rattle unconfident core beliefs.

Coaching yourself to more confidence means recognizing and acknowledging your talents, achievements and abilities. It means praising yourself and encouraging yourself, and these things begin to rattle low self-esteem; they begin to replace the negative beliefs with more positive ones.

As you do this, you will begin to shift from a negative attitude towards yourself to a neutral one. In this neutral place questions happen, you can think of your history and think, 'Yes, I am a good nurse/I am a good sister/I did do well in my degree' – whatever it might be. And that challenges those negatives beliefs, and gives your inner critic something to think about – and self-esteem begins in blossom.

As I said at the beginning, confidence is made up of competence and capability. You'll never believe you can be confident if you're constantly telling yourself you can't do things.

Fortunately, although it takes courage and effort, low self-esteem and the negative core beliefs that accompany it can be changed.

Symptoms of High Self-esteem

> believing in yourself
> accepting yourself, warts and all
> believing 'I can do this'
> trusting your intuition
> self-respect, respecting yourself

believing you can be a success

believing you can change

believing you can tackle the challenges life throws at you

feeling OK about change

believing you don't have to have a relationship for your life to be OK – you can survive as a single

feeling optimistic

being in touch with your emotions – not repressing them or blowing them up unnecessarily

valuing what *you* want and think over what *others* want and think

having an opinion

behaving decisively

being open

being assertive

saying no without fretting

being able to take risks

communicating clearly and effectively

liking your body and your image – even when it's not what the world deems 'perfect'

☆ Star Tip

The other thing to know about self-esteem is it is not constant. It see-saws up and down according to our circumstances and stress levels.

Exercise

Self-praise

Take the things you wrote down in the exercise from Chapter 1 (page 12) and give yourself a compliment for each one. For example:

'I am confident I can cook dinner.'

Could be complimented by:

'I am a good cook,' or even 'My food is as tasty as Nigella Lawson's.'

(Do have fun with this – it's not meant to be drudgery!)

Now score this exercise. How hard was it, out of 10? The higher your score, the higher your habit of self-criticism, lower your self-belief and the more you will benefit from the techniques in this book.

In Chapter 7 we'll look at how to take this further by working some more with the very powerful tool of affirmations.

5

Are You a Shy Baby?

I can't remember a time when I didn't feel shy; it's something I was no doubt born with. As genetic research suggests, some of us have a biological predisposition to timidity and excessive self-consciousness. My earliest memories have to do with being shy: visiting relatives and hiding behind my mother's legs; going to playgroup and clutching my twin sister's hand; my heart pounding with anxiety at the prospect of speaking in front of the class at school. Adolescence was a virtual blur of shyness …

Today I've outgrown the obvious symptoms of shyness – I don't shake or blush or stammer. I don't appear to be visibly frightened, but I haven't outrun the core feelings. Put me in a new social situation and my first, visceral reaction can be summed up in a word: Aargh!

Caroline Knapp, US writer for *Cosmopolitan*, on her history of shyness

Shyness is the reverse side of the confidence coin. When you're shy, you feel incapable of putting yourself forward. When you feel confident, you *do* feel capable. So shyness can hold you back. And although many of the elements of shyness are things we've already touched on, it's worth some space of its own.

Because the feeling of self-confidence is so subjective, it is notoriously hard to research. Much more work has been done on shyness.

Even so, statistics vary wildly. Lynne Crawford, who runs the London Shyness Centre, says '60 per cent of the population lives with shyness to varying degrees.' Other US-based research suggests that over the past two decades, the number of people who describe themselves as chronically shy has increased from 40 to 50 per cent, with most people becoming shy in specific situations (romantic and authority figures being major shyness-inducers). Research on children found 80 per cent feel shy sometimes, while 25 per cent are chronically shy and 4 per cent are shy and withdrawn constantly. And in the US, extreme shyness is labelled 'social anxiety disorder', which is said to be a severe psychological problem for 7 per cent of the population.

'Social anxiety disorder' is a fear of social situations involving interacting with other people. What singles sufferers out is their extreme fear of being judged and evaluated by others and their assumption that others are *always* viewing them harshly. Symptoms are triggered by factors like being the centre of attention, being observed while doing something, being teased or criticized and, especially, meeting and dealing with people in authority. And although that 7 per cent might have the worst of it, these situations (and situations where these factors tend to surface, like job interviews or dates) can get to most of us.

Fascinatingly, there does seem to be a genetic component governing whether we quiver or shine in social situations. Harvard psychologist Jerome Kagan discovered that shyness in adults could be traced back as far as toddlerhood and is associated with a different pattern of brain activity to non-shy individuals. He found sensitive and fearful children grow into shy and timid adults, and he reckoned they make up some 15 to 20 per cent of the population.

The Sad Repercussions of Shyness

As I said, shyness can hold you back from achieving your dreams and making the most of your life.

Research shows that shy people have more problems advancing on the job than those who can muster up some confidence. Studies at the University of Tulsa in the US found that the shyer the individual, the less prestigious his or her last job title tends to be. A 1998 US International Labor Office survey found shy people are more at risk from workplace bullying. Dr Jonathan Creek, author of *Conquering Shyness: The Battle Anyone Can Win*, says: 'Under-employment – being stuck in a job that requires less skill or training than you possess; uneasy work relationships and slower advancement mark the careers of shy people.'

The constant anxiety engendered by imagining everyone you meet is judging you harshly takes a heavy toll on the health and can lead to depression and even agoraphobia – fear of 'outside' places. Plus Kagan's research found timid children were more likely to experience panic attacks than their bolder classmates.

Shy people can also be, through no fault of their own, unpopular people. Symptoms of shyness – not making eye contact, not smiling, not speaking – can be perceived by others as being aloof, stuck-up, snobby, unfriendly. Caroline Knapp found this out when, after living next door to her neighbour for four years, she finally got to know her well enough to have coffee (they were both shy people). Their talk drifted to a party a group of people in their neighbourhood had held the year before in communal gardens. Caroline had skipped the party – 'far too daunting and scary' – but her neighbour knew her non-appearance was perceived as rude and that she was seen as rather superior and aloof. Caroline gasped, 'They think I'm aloof? Can't they tell I'm shy?' Apparently not. And as Caroline concludes: 'Shyness is a burden not just for the shy person, it also makes life difficult for the people around us.'

However, if you recall wetting the bed at the prospect of a birthday party and feel pretty much the same way now, be reassured that character is *not* destiny. All the researchers note that with a bit of work and practice, even extreme shyness can be overcome.

Factors like poise, self-confidence, verbal skills and feeling easy around others are bread and butter for getting ahead in the workplace, getting ahead in life. You owe it to yourself to build up your confidence, given that the alternative means hiding your talents under a bushel and living an unfulfilled and maybe unhappy life. As Caroline Knapp says, 'Social skills, it turns out, are like muscles, prone to atrophy if not used regularly. And when I don't use my social skills my natural shyness grows. And the world out there grows scarier.'

Tactics for Shy Babies

Do you believe people are constantly judging you harshly?

If so, just be aware it's only another of those negative beliefs that increase stress (see page 29) and *it ain't necessarily so*.

One of the simplest and most effective ways to bust this belief is to stop judging yourself so harshly. It worked for Jodie, 35, who says, 'I used to have a phobia about speaking in public. I had a good job where I had to do that occasionally and I used to find talking to any group excruciating. I couldn't stand being seen because I thought people would be criticizing and judging me. It was the same if I went to a party or room of people, I just knew they'd be looking me up and down and criticizing me. Recently I gave a speech at a friend's wedding and it went fine. And the reason I was able to do it is because now I don't feel that way any more. I can go in and be me and I like me. The other day I went to a business meeting dressed as myself for the first time in 15 years and it felt really good. I know it's a little thing, but it felt hugely significant. It felt such a relief.'

How did Jodie get to feel more accepting of herself? 'It was a gradual process. I had always secretly wanted to be an artist, and when I let myself start studying art – which took some time from starting out at an evening class and ending up going whole hog and going to art college – that really helped because I was accepting a part of me. Every day I came up against thoughts that said, "You'll never be good enough; who wants to see things you've made?" But I pushed on through and it had the wonderful side-effect of making me feel more confident and less hard on myself.'

According to the boffins, the most effective therapy for social anxiety disorder is participation in what's called an 'active behavioural therapy group' where people work on their fears in the group and get feedback from others about what people really think of them. You could try your own mini-version of this by asking friends for feedback. Find out if, really, they are judging you harshly.

The truth is that, yes, there will always be people who don't like you, or think that skirt you're wearing is hideous. And there will be people who love it. Jane, 27, says 'Now when I enter a party I remind myself that probably half the people in the room will be prettier than me, half may be cleverer than me, and the other half won't be. Somehow, this helps.'

Other things that help are cultivating listening skills. If you don't feel *you're* the wittiest person around, listening – making eye contact, smiling, asking questions – is a real ice-breaker. It avoids people forming those off-whack ideas that you're stand-offish or superior. Once you're confident you can do that, you're on your way.

NB: If shyness is a crippling problem for you, do see your GP about it. There are effective therapeutic techniques available and your GP could recommend you to a specialist. Why suffer in silence when you know there is help available?

Enough, Already!

That's enough about all these things that undermine your confidence. You know them now. Let's get on with the real, exciting work of tackling them and upping your confidence so that any minute there'll be no stopping you. This time next year you won't recognize yourself.

Time to work that confidence muscle …

Summary of Part One

▶ You no longer believe in myths about confidence – like some people have it and others don't.

▶ You know what confidence is: The belief you can handle people and situations, based on a sense of knowledge, competence and capability.

▶ You recognize in yourself the enemies of confidence: Fear, criticism, perfectionism, victim thinking and stress.

▶ You know that faulty beliefs increase stress and bring about wobbles in confidence.

▶ You understand the close connection between confidence and self-esteem, and how low self-esteem often rests on negative core beliefs we have about ourselves.

▶ You know whether you lack confidence or are just straight shy.

2

How to Coach
Yourself
Confident

6

Getting Started

So, how exactly do you coach yourself to become more confident? Now we'll look at the tips, tricks and techniques which will enable us to look and sound more confident, feel more confident, *be* more confident.

In this part, we're going to work with a case history of a woman I coached through a situation where she needed confidence. Her confidence wobbler happened at work, but the same guidelines apply to, say, telling your parents you're not coming home for Christmas, ending your relationship, informing your insolvent brother you're not going to bail him out any more, telling that moony guy who keeps giving you the hairy eyeball to back off, asking for a rise. In Part 3 we'll look at various situations in more detail, but for now we'll look at what happened to Margaret.

Margaret's Situation

I am a writer. My plan for my life was to become self-employed and work from home rather than get promoted through the ranks to boss. But then everything changed – I went for a job interview for the editorship of a monthly magazine and, to my utter surprise, was offered the job. Although the prospect of all that responsibility terrified me, I took it.

For the first time in my life, I was scared. I really thought I had bitten off more than I could chew. I also believed I didn't deserve the job. This was because of the circumstances surrounding the appointment. The position had arisen because the editor had died. For the past six months, the magazine had had an acting editor, who had applied for the editor's post. But instead of choosing him and employing an established member of staff, the company chose to employ me – a female twenty-something with no managerial experience. I felt I did not get the job because of my talents, but because they did not want to employ the acting editor. The acting editor then became my deputy, and to top it all, he turned out to be twice my age.

I am normally a very confident person, but in this situation I felt out of my depth. I desperately wanted everyone to like me, so I avoided making unpopular decisions. I allowed my deputy to undermine me and I didn't stand up for myself when dealing with him. Dealing with other people was not so much of a problem.

The turning point came when I had to tell my deputy he couldn't go to a conference in his favourite country, and that I was going instead. I tried to tell him several times, but he just wouldn't take in what I was trying to tell him. I gave all sorts of reasons and tried to justify myself, but each time I tried to get the message across, he managed to come up with a counter argument and the decision was delayed.

Then I had some training which involved role-play. I acted out this scenario with one of the other students, and our conversation was analysed. I was using typically weak phrases such as 'I think that it would be better if …' or 'Don't you think it would be better if …?' Instead, I was asked to think about the fact that I had a right to make unpopular decisions; that I had a right not to justify myself; and that I didn't have to be liked by everyone all the time. So, when it was time for the real thing I used the phrase 'I've made a decision. I'm going to the conference and you are staying in the office.' Finally, the message sunk in and he accepted my decision.

This might sound like just one small step, but for me it felt like a huge leap. I had crossed a line I had never crossed before. Next time it would be easier. Although this experience made me feel very proud of myself, I know similar situations will arise in the future and that each one will need to be tackled with conscious thought about my wording and behaviour. Then, hopefully, after much practice, asserting myself will come naturally. But for now I feel like a huge burden has been lifted from me. I feel I have gained control again. I feel a million times more confident.

Margaret's story illustrates several key points about confidence:

- ► It often wobbles when we take on a new challenge.
- ► It often wobbles when we feel out of our depth.
- ► It often wobbles when some belief about ourselves is exposed, some doubt about us is touched on (Margaret's doubt was whether she was really qualified for the job compared to the deputy's age and experience).
- ► The way we talk to ourselves doesn't help (Margaret telling herself she couldn't understand why she got the job – her age didn't bother her employers any).
- ► When we lack confidence we often speak in an unclear, apologetic way which makes us *sound* unconfident and comes across as not confident.
- ► We can change our words and behaviour to sound confident (even when we still aren't).

► This gets results (her deputy caved in when Margaret seemed sure).

► And makes us feel more confident about next time; therefore practice makes confident.

The other significant point about Margaret's story is, while she got help on one of my training courses and could role-play her difficult conversation there and get feedback, the rest of the group and I weren't there gunning for her when she actually tackled her deputy in real life. She had to get herself through that. She had to *coach* herself through that.

She did it – and so can you.

Let's take the elements which build confidence one by one. You coach yourself in each area, put them all together and – Eureka! – you won't recognize yourself. You'll make Sharon Stone look like a shrinking violet, make Britney Spears seem like a shybaby lightweight. Anything is possible when you know you have the tools to tackle any situation which might arise.

The confidence tool kit starts here.

Your Confident Body

We do not have bodies, we *are* our bodies. Emotional reality and biological ground are the same and cannot, in any way, be separated or distinguished.

Bodywork guru Stanley Keleman

Research into how we communicate reveals fascinating facts about how much the message we're putting across is conveyed by the words used, how much by our tone of voice and how much by body language. Statistics vary slightly, but hover around the fact that 7 per cent is words; 38 per cent is tone of voice, and 55 per cent body language.

The point here is just how much is conveyed non-verbally. If you're putting out an unconfident message with your body, it completely cancels out any bolshie-sounding words you might be using.

When we're anxious about something, we tend to focus on 'What will I *say*?' Unfortunately, we're missing most of the point.

Say you spot a guy in a bar trying to pick up a woman. He asks her if she wants a drink, she says, 'No thanks', but she smiles and turns her whole body towards him. He tries a different tack, 'Where are you from?' She answers, 'I don't want to tell you,' but again she smiles, makes direct eye contact with him.

Is this woman saying no, or is she flirting?

Say you're on a first date. You'd been eyeing this delicious speci-men for ages and you can't quite believe you're actually in the same room with him *on a date*! He's lovely, he's luscious and you have a creeping suspicion you might just have met the father of your future children. So, not to put too fine a point on it, you are scared shitless. You want to flirt, want to come across as a sassy, sussed and Not At All Scared sex monster. But the fear is making you contort and slump, you're breathing quicker than a stop-watch on overdrive, fearful thoughts whizz through your brain like meteorites on a mission. All this mental activity and hyper-ventilating creates that slightly out-of-your body spacey feeling. Like you're not really here but watching yourself in a movie.

A question: *How will you appear to him?*

Now imagine that just for one second you remember to take a deep breath and feel your feet on the floor at the same time. Immediately your body starts to calm down – a deep breath gives it the message 'OK, panic over, nothing to worry about.' And you can't keep thinking wild thoughts because all your attention is focused on just noticing your feet. Your feet enjoy this attention and, like magic, this brings your centre of gravity down and the spaciness begins to dissipate. You might even relax enough to smile at the poor guy. (Who is probably just as nervous himself. Ask him.)

So not only does our body language tell others more than we want them to know about how we *really* are, your body also speaks to you. Just standing up in a confident pose makes you feel 10 times more sure of yourself. Try it. Sit or stand up straight, head up. Make eye contact with yourself in the mirror and notice how you feel.

Try this: Imagine you're attempting a terrifying situation, like asking your boss for a pay rise. Now slump your shoulders forward, put your feet close together and assume the fig leaf position, hands over crotch. Notice how vulnerable you feel? This shows how posture dictates your state of mind. Now roll back your shoulders, unlock your knees, stand with your feet hip-width apart and let your arms hang at your sides or clasp your hands behind you. Now you look and feel like you mean business.

☆ **Star Tip**

Feeling your feet on the floor really works. As Maria, another delegate in one of my training courses puts it, 'I couldn't believe something so simple and easy-sounding could work so well. But I tried it during a difficult phonecall and it really worked. I was amazed.'

Confidence = Breathing

The other thing we do when we're even slightly scared is we breathe quickly and shallowly. And only in our upper chest, not deep into our lungs. This quick high breathing sends a message to your body to contract even more, breathe even quicker and more shallowly (it's that ancient 'fight or flight' fear response which evolved to ready us for running from sabre-toothed tigers).

Anyone who's had the misfortune to have a panic attack will know how, in the throes of one of these, you really feel like you're dying. That's how extreme fear can feel. That's what fear can do to your body.

But if you can re-organize your body to breathe more deeply and slowly (which, by magic, you already do when you stand up straighter, drop your shoulders back and allow the thorax more room), instantly you'll feel better.

☆ Star Tip
Feelings follow behaviour.

There's a saying psychotherapists use: feelings follow behaviour. It's true. Standing up straight in a confident body is a simple, instant piece of behaviour you can do anywhere, any time.

When Margaret (from page 63) first sat down that day on the training course to try out her role-play, the minute she eyeballed the trainee playing her awkward deputy her breathing sped up.

This made her voice sound wobbly. She also bent forward in a tense, earnest pose which screamed 'I'm not sure about this so I'm going to work really hard to get my message across.'

So, before she even got to the point, I stopped her and coached her to sit back, feel her feet on the floor, breathe deeper and take her time.

It worked. As Margaret says 'I couldn't believe what a difference just sitting up and breathing differently made. I suddenly felt surer.'

Exercise

Find Your Confident Body

Stand up straight. You may want to play around a bit, stamp your feet into the floor, shake the tension out of your hands, consciously free the muscles in your neck.

And really inhabit it. Feel how your knees are, feel your feet on the floor, notice where your shoulders are.

Once you, as Madonna would say, 'strike the pose', tell yourself to remember it. Tell yourself you can access this pose, this body, any time you're feeling less than confident, and know that just this alone will help. It will remind you you can look, feel confident.

> ▶ *You're the coach! Remember that, coach! Whenever you're in a situation where you need to draw on inner supplies of confidence, use this body – and breathe!*

Try it out:

The proof of the pudding is in the eating. The way to try all these tools is give them a go in the real world. This is a relatively simple one. You can walk to the bus-stop using your confident body. Sit and eyeball your boss doing it, use it the next time that annoying bod from department groan approaches you. The more you practise accessing your confident body, the more it will become second nature. And you can't possibly lose.

Breathing deeply is good for you anyway. When we only use the upper part of our lungs, toxic residues are not completely removed. Breathing deeply is a stress-busting technique that relaxes you anywhere.

7

Being Your Own
Confidence Coach

Treat yourself as a true friend and your journey through life will
be pleasant and rewarding.
Dr Brian Roet, psychologist

I do say things to myself which, if a friend or acquaintance said
them, I'd be insulted and outraged … Well, now I'm stopping
all that. Now I really listen to [the positive things] my friends
say and say similar things to myself when I start feeling and
thinking negatively.
Miranda, on tackling her inner critic

'You've got spots, fat ankles and no one likes you.' If you had a
friend who talked to you this way you'd ditch her quicker than
you could splutter the words 'How dare you?' Yet every day you
say things just as cruel to someone you're supposed to really care
about – you.

It's that inner critic, giving you a hard time. Now it's time for the
antidote, time for the inner critic to meet its nemesis: the inner
best friend, who doubles as your very own confidence coach.

Being your own best friend is the way to drown out the chatter
of the inner critic and adjust any thoughts of low self-worth that
surface when the odd negative belief is triggered.

Think about the vicious rantings of your inner critic, your put-down thoughts, as the croakings of your inner enemy. Imagine you also have an inner hero, an inner best friend who can counteract all that.

First, though, you have to accept that you are responsible for the way you think, feel and talk to yourself. You're responsible for how you react to people and events. And that your attitudes and actions have consequences.

The concept of an inner enemy and inner best friend is not something I made up for fun. It comes from what's called cognitive therapy – literally re-training the mind to think differently and more positively.

When you tell yourself off, stop and ask, what's the evidence for that? Or what would be the worst thing if it were true? Are you over-generalizing and making everything about yourself wrong just because you made some innocent mistake?

Doing this is both difficult and easy. Easy because it's pretty straightforward to think what a best friend would say in certain circumstances; difficult because old habits die hard. But changing old habits is what this book is about – and what you'll have to do if you want to feel supreme self-confidence.

Here are some examples.

You Say	**Your Best Friend Says**
'I'm so stupid, God I'm stupid.'	'With a job like yours you sure aren't stupid.'

You Say	**Your Best Friend Says**
'I never do anything right. I'm so clumsy.'	'It's not like you burnt the house down.'
'I'll never meet anyone again.'	'I'm sure the love of your life is just round the corner.'
'Why do I waste time going to interviews? I'll never get the job. I don't think I'll even apply.'	'What have you got to lose? If you don't get this job, you'll get a better one.'
'I look like Melvyn Bragg in a hurricane.'	'Your hair is so thick and shiny.'
'I always pick the wrong moment to row with my man.'	'And relationship counsellors don't? Say sorry over dinner.'
'That job's finished now, I'll start on the next task.'	'You did that really well, you should be proud of yourself.'
'I hate myself.'	'Oh really? So that's why you bought that dress that makes you look like a goddess.'
'Oh all right, I suppose I do quite like myself.'	'You're a really good person, sweetie.'

There is sometimes a (teensy) grain of truth in what the inner critic says. But it comes all dressed up like a Halloween horror. Like, 'You made a mistake. You're a stupid, stupid failure and you'll probably get the sack.'

When you hear your inner critic begin to rant, say to yourself: 'STOP.' Ask yourself: 'Is there some truth in the inner critic's message?' Acknowledging some truth, like 'Yes, I did make a mistake' often helps it shut up faster. Then ask, 'What would my best friend say?' Which would be something like: 'Yes, you made a mistake but it's not the end of the world. You're still a capable person, you just made a mistake. Get over it.'

Being your own best friend is part of being your own confidence coach. It is all about learning the art of self-encouragement.

☆ Star Tip

Your inner critic will never entirely go away (inasmuch as nothing in our personalities ever entirely goes away), but if you practise the art of being your own best friend it may appear less often, or will soften. There WILL be an improvement.

Remember Margaret? Our case history from the beginning of Part Two?

Her own inner critic was giving her a hard time before the training course by telling her her deputy was better qualified to do the job than she was. I don't know the exact words it used, but the effect was to make her feel small and unqualified and unworthy before a man who was older than her. Practising her conversation with us in the training room helped her encourage herself: she knew she could do it because she'd done it with us. Even so, she had to keep reminding herself she could do it when we weren't there.

Exercise

What would your best friend say about some of your own individual favourite put-downs? What does she say when you're down and dreary? What would you like her to say?

Use the affirmation: *'I can be my own best friend. I can coach myself to confidence.'*

Your Shiny New Confident Beliefs

Before a date or job interview or even just a night out, my mind races with self-doubt. So I look in the mirror and tell myself: 'I am hot stuff. I *am* hot stuff. I'm *really* hot stuff.' It makes me laugh and gives me killer confidence.

Nina, 26, accountant

Remember how we said negative beliefs about yourself drag you down? Time to give them an overhaul. Right now you can start digging them out and replacing them with bright, shiny, happy, healthy new ones. Try these on for size:

> 'I believe in myself.'
> 'I trust my own instincts.'
> 'I am a confident person.'
> 'I am OK, exactly as I am.'
> 'I have a nice body.'
> 'I look good.'
> 'I look just fine.'
> 'I am an attractive woman.'
> 'I am good enough.'
> 'I am competent and intelligent.'

> 'I can speak up for myself.'
> 'I am capable of taking on challenges.'
> 'I can change.'
> 'The world is on my side.'
> 'I am popular and other people like me.'
> 'I am a good person.'

How would you feel if you believed all those? On top of the world, right?

If you truly held these beliefs at the core of your being, when bad things happened you might wobble a bit but you wouldn't fall to pieces.

One of the best and easiest ways to replace old beliefs with new ones is using the tool of affirmations.

They will feel silly at first. You will feel daft doing them. If you really want to change, though, you *will* keep doing them. They will work.

Some more examples:

> 'I love my body.'
> 'I love and accept myself in every way.'
> 'I am competent and confident.'
> 'All my communications are clear, witty and direct.'
> 'I am loving and lovable.'

Don't forget the rights from Chapter 3. Remember which ones were revelations for you?

I   I have the right to ask for what I want (realizing the other person has the right to say 'No'.)

2   I have the right to have opinions, feelings and emotions and to express them appropriately.

3   I have the right to make statements which have no logical basis and which I don't have to justify (e.g. intuitive ideas and comments).

4   I have the right to make my own decisions and to cope with the consequences.

5   I have the right to choose whether or not to get involved in someone else's problems.

6   I have the right not to know about something and not to understand.

7   I have the right to make mistakes.

8   I have the right to be successful.

9   I have the right to change my mind.

10   I have the right to privacy.

11   I have the right to be alone and independent.

12   I have the right to change myself and to act differently/confidently.

If you have trouble even imagining you could believe these things, affirm:

'I am willing to change' or *'I am willing to change my beliefs to positive ones.'*

☆ Star Tip

It helps to speak these positive statements out loud to yourself in front of the mirror. It has a deadly effect on old, worn-out negative beliefs.

Useful Confident Beliefs

I can be confident.

I am confident.

Other people are safe to be around.

Other people are judging me neutrally.

Other people are not better or worse than me, they are just human.

I am willing to change and be confident.

I am becoming more confident with every day that passes.

Exercise

Your Precious Bag of Compliments

Think of compliments you've been given in your life, both recently and in the past. Write all these compliments down on separate pieces of paper. Do 20, then do another 20. Think of compliments you've received at work, about your clothes or appearance, from lovers past and present, from friends. Then think of 20 compliments you received as a child.

When you have a pile of compliments, put them somewhere special. Either decorate a large envelope or make or buy a wonderful bag you can get out and look at. Or buy or decorate a box. The beauty of the container is supposed to reflect the preciousness of the contents.

Now you have your precious bag of compliments. But don't just let them languish. Get them out and look at them at least once a week while you're working with this book. Get them out and look at them before you're about to take on anything challenging. Get them out and read them when you feel low and worthless.

Reading them over and over, knowing they're true, will help you through and build your confidence, like they did for Marion, who says, 'I have a friend who made me a wonderful pink purse for me to put my compliments in. She helped me remember the things I've been complimented on, and added a few as we went along. Now, whenever I have to do a presentation at work, which I do often have to do and which gives me the collywobbles, I get out the purse the night before and read them all. Sometimes I even take out a few slips of paper and put them in my pocket. It may sound silly, but it really helps.'

8

Your Confident
Communications

It's not what you say, it's the way that you say it.

Communication is a crucial element of confidence. When we
don't feel sure of ourselves we twist ourselves in knots worrying,
'How can I say this?' 'How can I turn that nasty task down?' 'Should
I have said that?'

When we're not confident it shows up in our speech, our voice,
our words.

Communication is our interface with the world. It's a crucial part
of the image we project. As we know from Chapter 1, confidence
is made up of knowledge, competence and capability. Here's all
you need to know about sounding – and therefore appearing –
confident.

Weeding Out Unconfident Words

First step is to do a little weeding. Any and all of the following
statements make you sound about as self-assured as a priest at a
dating agency. Even when you *feel* confident, these things let you
down.

Apologizing	'Sorry to bother you,' 'Sorry to have to say this,' 'I'm sorry to say,' 'I hate to say this …'
Blathering	'You probably won't want to hear this, but …'
Stalling	'Er, um, you know.'
Qualifiers	'I'm a little bit angry'; 'I'd just like you to do this little bit of work.'
Asking permission	'Could I just say …?' 'Don't you agree that …?'

All these things water down your communication. Clear communication equals confident communication (and vice versa).

Remember Margaret saying she'd tried telling her deputy she didn't want him to go to the conference? She'd said, 'Don't you think it would be better if I went?' Of course he didn't. Phrases like these water down our message.

Recognize yourself here? If Yes, try the exercise below.

If No, move on to 'Tone of Voice', after the exercise.

I've said it before, and I'll say it again:

Awareness is the first step towards change.

So. If you notice yourself doing these things, DON'T beat yourself up. Think of this knowledge as the tool you need in order to change.

Exercise

Tape yourself, or ask friends for feedback. Ask them to score you 1 to 10 on how confident you sound. Then practise in front of the mirror.

Tone of Voice: How to Sound Assured

Now to look at (or, rather, hear) tone of voice. Do people who cold-call ask to speak with your mother? 'A high-pitched, nasal voice sounds whiny and irritating,' says Dorothy Sarnoff, a communications coach. 'It's an ineffective style of speech.'

It always amazes me how many people say 'Is that me?' or 'I can't stand the sound of my own voice' when I'm taping and playing back their interviews. Why not?

Think how Margaret Thatcher changed her vocals to sound more authoritative by dropping the pitch a couple of octaves.

To sound more authoritative, lower your voice pitch. Place your hand on your chest and lower your voice until you can actually feel the vibrations from the words, then speak from there.

Tape yourself to find which parts of your voice need working on – pitch, tone, intonation, a tendency to say 'ummm,' 'yeah' or 'you know' or to lengthen certain vowels.

If you know you go off and start squeaking there are two ways to go with this:

1   Learn to love your own voice.

2   Do something about it (speech therapist, voice coach – ask your GP or look in your local directory).

But really, the crucial point is: when you whine, when you plead, when you sound unconfident, you *are* unconfident.

Getting Clear

When you're clear about what you're saying, you automatically sound more confident. So let's look at how you can do this.

Most of us can rabbit on regardless when we feel relaxed. These tips are designed for when you need to transmit a certain message that you feel anxious about. Like complaining in a shop. Or saying no to a date. Or asking your boss for a promotion. Or telling your parents something they don't want to hear. Or dealing with put-downs or disrespect. Or ending a relationship. Or job interviews. Or talking with your doctor or anyone intimidating in authority. Or standing up for yourself with that friend who bosses you. Or asking for help.

Getting Your Message Across

Define Your Purpose

The key to confident communication is simplicity itself. All you have to do is define your central message, then stick to it, repeat it and don't be deflected from your purpose.

This is what Margaret did in her difficult conversation with her deputy. She defined her purpose as: 'I need to tell him that he's not going to the conference and I'm going instead.'

Confident Things to Remember When Communicating

You don't have to justify yourself, blather on, give a hundred reasons.

Don't fuss or worry about the person you're communicating with.

Do make eye contact.

Don't keep adjusting your message to what you think they want to hear.

Don't change your tune just because they disagree.

Don't disarm compliments. Say thank you and move on.

Ask questions. Focusing on the other person helps you worry less about you. This is a good tactic for parties. As one of my old bosses used to say, 'Ego always gets the better of caution.' People adore talking about themselves.

But what happens after that? As Rosa says, 'I can be clear about what I want to say, but then when I actually get in a conversation the other person says things which knock me sideways.' To help with this, we need a little science …

Transactional Analysis: A Way of Looking at Our Conversations

At this point it is useful to look at a communication model which will help you be more confident in your interactions with other people. 'Transactional analysis' is the bit-of-a-mouthful name for this system devised by Eric Berne.

Berne reckoned the personality is made up of three distinct parts or what he called 'ego states'. He looked at the transactions that take place between people and decided that people typically tend to come from one of these three separate places within their personalities when they're talking. They are:

1   The parent

2   The child

3   The adult.

1 When We Come from Our Parent

When in 'parent mode' we tend to transmit messages we heard our own parents or parental figures make when we were growing up. Our inner parent place is the receptacle for all the 'shoulds' and 'oughts' and laws we had around us when we were children. Like those moments when your flatmate has trashed the joint and as you are ticking her off you're thinking, 'My God, I sound just like my mother.' That's because you have flipped into parent. It *is* like you're replaying a tape of your own mother in tick-off mode.

Clues We Are in Parent

Abundant use of the words 'should' and 'ought'; furrowed brow, pursed lips, dramatic, apocalyptic statements like 'I'm going to put a stop to this once and for all ...', 'Never in all my days ...' 'Always' and 'never' are nearly always parent clue words.

There are two parent modes: Critical parent and Nurturing parent.

Critical Parent

The Critical parent stance tends to be, as the name suggests, critical and judgemental, full of anger and put-downs. It makes the receiver feel hopeless and helpless. When we talk to *ourselves* from critical parent, it is with the voice of the inner critic. This is where it comes from.

Nurturing Parent

The Nurturing parent is softer, kinder but still has a stance of 'Let me do it all for you,' 'Let me tell you what to do,' and 'I know better than you.' Which ALSO makes the recipient feel hopeless and helpless. When we're talking to ourselves, however, Nurturing parent is a good one to cultivate. If our real-life parents weren't especially nurturing, we may have to teach ourselves how to do it from scratch.

2 When We Come from Our Child

In child mode we speak and act – yes! – childishly. The child ego state is a carryover from our own childhood.

Clues We Are in Child

Because we first responded to the world in non-verbal ways, a lot of child clues are non-verbal, as in pouting, sulking, giggling, the quivering lip, foot-stomping temper tantrums – and so on. Verbal clues are using babytalk or whining, saying things like 'I want', 'I won't' or superlatives like 'biggest', 'bestest' or just 'wow'. Wrinkling your nose. Putting your hand in front of your mouth and gasping. You know the kind of thing.

There are three child modes: Rebellious child, Adaptive child and Free child.

Rebellious Child

Rebellious child tends to act out, slam doors and generally tell others where to get off. 'I won't' and 'Make me' are the battle cries of Rebellious child.

Adaptive Child

Adaptive child is the state that thinks, 'If I sit here and be good and quiet nothing bad will happen to me.' It is called 'adaptive' because it reflects a way of adapting to the demands of adults by being quiet and well behaved.

Free Child

Free child is the best of the child: playful, funny, creative.

The way your own individual child is will be influenced by the way you behaved as a child. If you were the rebel, you'll still feel like slamming doors when your boss has a go at you now. If you were well-behaved, the adaptive child could be how you are when you go into your inner child now.

NB Any kind of emotion will send us into our child ego state. That explains why people behave so childishly when they're in the grip of any strong feeling. Depending on what happened to us as children, the child can feel scared and unconfident. That explains why we often feel unconfident once strong emotions kick in.

3 When We Come from Our Adult

We are straight. We shoot from the hip. The adult is a mature and rational part of our personality. When we are listening without criticism, when we speak without putting the other person down, without appearing superior or inferior or childish, we are in adult. Also, WE APPEAR CONFIDENT.

Clues We Are in Adult

Adult words are 'When', 'why', 'where', 'who', 'what' and 'how'. The adult asks lots of questions, mulls them over and gives sane, clear responses. Things like 'I think that …' 'I see' and 'In my opinion …' The adult offers suggestions without making the other person feel bad: 'What you could do is …' And the adult can laugh and joke like the child without 'acting up'. The adult can have the best parts of the parent and child. In the famous book on transactional analysis, this is the ego state that gave the book its title: *I'm OK, You're OK*.

Neither the parent nor child is 'bad' per se. Two people in 'parent' at a bus-stop could happily moan about the world for hours. And sometimes a good old parental moan does us good. Sometimes it's useful to be judgemental, to 'put people in their place', to inhabit the moral high ground, to be able to say *How dare you?* And the Free child is where our creativity comes from. It's also fun to be in child – playing around, say, when making love or with real children. The trick lies in knowing when to use which ego state. And having a healthy adult part we can access when we need to.

☆ **Star Tip**

Operating from the adult position stops us acting like a victim, just as being our own best friend cancels out victim thinking.

How Will This Help My Confidence?

Knowing we have an adult part that can respond appropriately to any situation (we'll look at how in a minute) is an invaluable resource. You can coach yourself confident from adult (and hopefully have fun with it from child). Your adult part is realistic. Change and growth can come from here. We never change or grow when we're stuck with childish responses or re-running old tapes of what our parents said to us.

A Guide to Adult (and Confident) Language

Adult language is …

▶   clear – avoiding all those qualifications, apologies and blathering we looked at earlier
▶   direct – doesn't beat around the bush. A simple message is best because there's less room for the listener to misunderstand or switch off.
▶   specific – vague language is meaningless language. Even when it's complimentary. If your boss tells you you're doing a wonderful job, it's nice, but it doesn't tell you what, specifically, he's noticed. Whereas, 'You got that report done in record time and it reads really well' says so much more. It says he's truly seen you and noticed what you've done. It's the same in love. I had a partner once who was loving, but I never knew what he loved about me. He never took the time (or

bothered – I'm not sure which) to say. My next
boyfriend was very good at noticing small things and
appreciating them. For the first time in years, I felt like
a princess.

▶ focused on you rather than the other person. So not:
'You're a lazy sod' but 'I feel really angry when the
house is untidy.' Adult language makes abundant use of
the 'I' word: I see, I would like, I think, I feel that . . .

▶ looking for solutions – in his best-seller *I'm OK, You're
OK*, author Thomas Harris says the basic vocabulary of
the adult consists of 'why, what, where, when, who and
how'.

▶ focused on someone's *behaviour*, not their personality.
This is a neat trick which makes other people much
less likely to take things badly. So, once again, not
'You're a lazy sod' but 'You've been half an hour late
every day this week.'

▶ rational, realistic, and doesn't slag off, go below the
belt or insult

▶ sure it's got its facts right. How does the other person
see the problem? Why did they do what they did?
Often we make assumptions about what something's
about, but there's no substitute for hearing from the
source. Asking for clarification or summarizing back to
the other person what they've said makes people
know you've listened and helps you check you've got
things straight.

▶ not afraid to ask for time to think, or take time to
speak. Nor does it get critical or mess about.

▶ attentive. The adult also *listens*. Using eye contact,
nodding and other visual signals shows you're listening.

▶ *honest* without being tactless. The adult confidently
knows you have the right to speak without constantly

worrying how your message will be received by
others. That's *their* business.

**Remember Margaret and her tricky conversation with
her deputy?**

She used clear, adult conversation by defining her central message, which was: 'I've made a decision. I'm going to the conference
and you are staying in the office.'

Of course her deputy tried a few detracting tactics, a few 'Yes,
buts …,' but Margaret showed in her body language, her tone of
voice and what she said, using adult language so the conversation
couldn't go off into parent or child, that she meant business.

A Guide to Being 'In Adult'

What Works	What Doesn't
Thinking before you speak	Flying off the handle
Being specific	Being vague/unclear/using generalities ('You never …')
Focusing on you	Focusing on the other person
Focusing on behaviour	Focusing on personality ('you slob')
Asking for what you want	Telling them what to do

Exercise

Think about some common over-and-over difficult communications you have with those closest to you – your best friend, your partner, your work colleagues, your family. What part are you playing in them?:

> Critical parent
> Nurturing parent
> Rebellious child
> Adaptive child
> Free child

What would it be like to be 'in adult' in these interactions? What would you say then? Go on, what would you *actually* say?

Pick one and have a practice in real life. Have fun with this – only you know you're doing it and trying something different. Watch what happens.

Exercise

Practising the Adult

Think of some statements you'd like to make to people in your life. Think about the way you usually say them (if you say them at all!), then how you might say them in adult.

Then actually try some adult conversations, delivering adult messages, out there in the world. Try them in less charged situations first – the ticketmaster at the station, the boy in the sandwich shop. This gets you confident you can do them before you try them with the people who matter.

9

Handling Difficult
Conversations Confidently

When I was young, whenever I had a negative feeling like anger or sadness, my mother would say 'Don't start.' And I learned not to start. I learned to hold all my feelings in. One of the effects of this on my life was that I let people walk all over me, because I'd got so used to not showing my anger. Then I began to notice that, in the workplace, 'not starting' wasn't doing me any favours. So I had to learn to 'start' from scratch. It felt massively scary at first. But I found that after I'd shown my anger, after I'd criticized someone positively, I'd feel so good and the negative feeling would float away. And that payoff – that good feeling – helped me continue. I'd be lying if I said I enjoy being angry or criticizing people, but I have at least learned how to do it.

Rosa, 34

Dealing with Criticism and Conflict

How do you deal with criticism? (Be honest now – no one's looking.)

☐ Act defensively   ☐ Ask for justification

☐ Respond with anger   ☐ Look for the truth in what
  or attack   they say

☐ Deny everything   ☐ Admit my mistake

☐ Criticize in return   ☐ Attempt to solve the
                                              problem

☐ Retreat   ☐ State my opinion

☐ Sulk   ☐ Know when it's unfair and
                                              therefore don't take it on

How do you give criticism?

☐ I don't, I avoid the issue   ☐ Get to the point

☐ Drop hints   ☐ Concentrate on facts

☐ Send a memo/write a letter   ☐ Ignore emotional reactions

☐ Moan about it to others   ☐ Look ahead to a solution
   and hope it'll get back to
   the person

☐ Try to soften the criticism,   ☐ Say what I would like instead
   watering it down

☐ Accept excuses   ☐ Accept any criticism/
                                              feedback due in return

☐ Offer 'friendly' advice

There's no right and wrong, but there are tactics with criticism –
both the giving and receiving of it – which work more effectively
than others. The key is, the reactions on the right of the above
quiz are more effective and likely to yield positive results than the
ones on the left.

The reactions on the left tend to compound the problem and can lead to blow-ups or 'unfinished business' (to use that horrible psychobabbly phrase) which leaves things up in the air and emotions hanging about and festering, rather than being 'out there' and dealt with.

The reactions on the right are more effective, more likely to deal with the issue and 'finish' it and more confident. Although, of course, it takes more confidence to have the responses on the right. It's easier to avoid a problem than to confront it. Often people who lack confidence doubt their own responses: 'I'm angry with Jo but I haven't really a right to this anger, it's silly, and therefore I'd better shut up.' Does this make the anger go away? No. And the next time Jo repeats the kind of behaviour you were angry with her about, you'll feel twice as angry because the previous, un-dealt-with anger is still hanging about.

The consequences of withholding criticism:

▶   The emotion festers – and there is abundant evidence about the consequences to your health of repressed emotions like anger.
▶   You don't get to practise speaking up for yourself, which is a vital part of becoming more confident.
▶   When you speak your truth you are effectively saying 'I matter,' and this builds your self-esteem. Not only does it give the message to others that you and your feelings matter, it also gives that message to *you*.

Some tips for receiving criticism:

▶   Breathe.
▶   Keep calm.

▶   Ask yourself, is it true?
▶   Don't take it personally – often criticism says more about the other person and whatever's going on for them (jealousy, a bad mood, PMT, negativity) than what's going on with you.
▶   Keep it light – don't fly off the handle.
▶   If it might be constructive criticism, ask questions: 'In what way am I letting the team down?' and get the other person to be specific: 'Can you give me an example of that?'
▶   And …

☆ Star Tip
Agree with the persecutor.

A bitchy colleague walks into your office and says: 'My God, what a hell hole. I'm amazed you can work in this mess.'

You say: 'Yes, it *is* really messy. It is amazing I can get any work done.'

This completely takes the wind out of her sails. And sounds a million times more confident than a defensive reaction like, 'What do you mean?' or an attacking 'Well, your desk is no better.'

Some tips for delivering criticism:

▶   Be specific.
▶   Don't slag the other person off or deliver sweeping put-downs.
▶   Focus on the behaviour, not the person.
▶   And …

☆ Star Tip
The Complaints and Recommendations Structure

A complaint without a recommendation is known as moaning: 'You never wash up.' Moaning – and its ugly sister, nagging – famously get you nowhere. All they achieve is to make you feel like a moan or a nag, and that, like any kind of self-criticism, erodes your self-esteem (and therefore confidence). They don't do you any favours with the person on the receiving end, either.

Recommendations do. They accentuate the positive and force the person delivering them (you) to be specific about what you want. It also leaves the receiver in no doubt about what you want and encourages them to take more responsibility for either doing it or not doing it.

The structure has three stages:

| 1 | The complaint: 'My complaint is you leave all your dirty crockery around the house and you don't wash up.' |

| 2 | The effects of this behaviour: 'I'm spending a lot of time doing both our shares of washing up and I'm getting resentful.' |

| 3 | Your recommendation: 'I want you to wash up after yourself, please.' |

It helps to get the other person to listen to the whole thing. So, ask permission: 'I'd like to talk to you about the washing up. Have you got a minute to listen?' (If they don't listen, or they interrupt, you'll have to ask them confidently to hear you out.)

☆ **Star Tip**

Try and get an **agreed** solution. Agreed solutions are far more likely to work than ones you impose on others.

Exercise

Construct some complaint and recommendation procedures around the following:

▶ Your flatmate won't wash up.
▶ Your boyfriend keeps arranging to go out with his mates without telling you.
▶ Your mother is much more financially generous with your sister than with you.
▶ A colleague keeps interrupting whenever you speak up in meetings.

When you've got the hang of it, think of three situations in your life you could currently make a complaint and recommendation about. What outcome do you really want? What change in others' behaviour do you really want to see? Try and focus on the positive.

Remember, others may not change – indeed, they have the right not to agree – but at least you've stated your recommendation.

Don't Say It Once Then Give In

You may have to make your point more than once. Although saying it at all might have been a big deal to you, the other person may not even have registered it. Sometimes people don't listen. Sometimes they simply don't realize you mean business.

Confidence can mean repeating yourself. But, once you've said it once, you have the experience of saying it. You know you can say it again.

Further Techniques for Difficult Conversations
Broken Record

Broken record is a technique which helps you:

▶   keep asserting your point
▶   not take no for an answer.

It's simple and easy to remember even in the most stressful situations. In fact it's a brilliant technique for stressful situations because it is so simple: you just keep repeating yourself. The technique is called 'broken record' because when using it you sound like a record stuck in its groove, repeating the same phrase over and over.

The theory behind the technique says that a human being cannot hear the same thing more than three times without caving in – or backing off; 99 per cent of people cave in after three repeats!

Either way, it's a crucial technique for getting what you want – confidently.

The trick lies in coming up with a key phrase which gets to the crux of your point.

Let's say you have a complaint to make against your friend. She keeps letting you down, cancelling at the last moment and generally behaving flakily. Your core statement could be:

'I'm angry that you keep cancelling at the last moment and I'd like it if you would stick to our arrangements. I want you to only make arrangements you can keep.'

The first time you make this statement she's going to say. 'Oh, but I'm so busy … blah blah blah'. You say: 'Yes, I hear you're busy and I'm angry that you keep cancelling. Please only make arrangements with me you can keep.'

Then she might come back with something like, 'Why are you having a go at me? You cancelled once.' In which case you say: 'I'm having a go because I'm angry you keep cancelling. I want you to stick to our arrangements.'

The technique works in many situations. It's good to acknowledge the sentiment of the other person's statement, but keep repeating your own.

It's good for complaining in a shop.

You say: 'This jumper shrank the first time I washed it and I want my money back.'

They say: 'I can't do that, madam. It's against company policy.'

You say: 'I hear it's against your policy but it's useless and I want my money back.'

They say: 'Wool does shrink sometimes. We can't give you your money back.'

You say: 'I know wool shrinks, but I followed the instructions on the label and it still shrank and I want my money back.'

The shop assistant is bound to cave in at this and at least get the manager, in which case you start broken record all over again with them.

Either way, you do not give in. You keep making your point.

▶   Margaret used the broken record technique with her deputy – she only had to repeat her core phrase: 'I've made a decision. I'm going to the conference and you are staying in the office' once (i.e. she said it twice altogether) and he caved in.

Saying No

Sarah, 25, a marketing executive, says: 'The higher I go up the career ladder, the more demands are made on my time, including social time with launches, client parties and so on. I had to learn how to say no, and it wasn't easy; saying no wasn't much of an option in my family. But I realized if I carried on saying yes to everything I would go pop. Now I still feel uncomfortable about saying no – my first instinct is still always to help – but I'm getting OK and it and the rewards are wonderful. More time for me!'

We often get ourselves into sticky situations by saying yes to things we don't really want to do. We often feel guilty if we say no. Yet saying no is often the confident option.

If you are a 'yesaholic' – you say yes as a knee-jerk reaction without really thinking about it – you could have fun with practising saying no. At the very least:

☆ Star Tip

Every single time you're asked to do something, ask for time.

- ▶ Practise saying no for the sake of it.
- ▶ You may have to use broken record. If, in the past, people have been used to you saying yes, they may try to persuade you back to the 'norm'.
- ▶ Make sure you believe in your right to say no – some people have a mistaken belief that their role in life is to be continually running around after others. But this only keeps them stuck and leads to stress and burn-out.
- ▶ Assertiveness training helps you practise saying no. There are many classes around the country, including night-school classes. Check out what's available in your local area.

Remember: you don't have to justify yourself. Confident people trust their feelings, their needs, and therefore their statements.

Things to Remember During Conflicted Conversations

- ▶ It's not all your fault.
- ▶ You don't have to apologize if it's not your fault.
- ▶ You don't have to justify yourself.
- ▶ You don't have to think of a million reasons why you did that or can't do this. That *is* justifying yourself.
- ▶ You don't have to take any shit – any insults, put-downs or other unpleasantness.
- ▶ You can't afford to spend all your energy worrying about other people and what they want or think about you. Just take care of yourself and they'll take care of their end of it.

Yes, they may not like you in this conversation. Shit happens. The world will not end.

They're not right about everything/better than you. You don't have to keep on arguing for hours and going round and round in circles. It's OK to say, 'I've had enough now, let's talk about it another time' (and make a date for when that another time will be).

10

Your Confident Behaviour

Just Do It!

Most people say to themselves, 'I need to feel confident, then I'll go out into the world and get a new job.' It actually works the other way around. Confidence comes from competence – if you can do something well, you're confident about it. But you only get good at something with practice. So, to get confident, you need to practise – whether it's meeting people, speaking in public, managing others or being a parent – you can't wait until you're confident to do it. Do it and you'll become confident.
Michael Maynard, founder of management consultants Maynard Leigh Associates, who lists Hewlett Packard, Airmiles and the London Stock Exchange among his blue-chip clients

Mike has put his finger on one of the major paradoxes about confidence. The lack of it holds us back, but actually the only way to get it is to pinch a tick from Nike's slogan and Just Do It.

All the experts agree that confidence doesn't just arrive out of nowhere. It comes from building on past successes. You can read this book and know all there is to know about confidence, but unless you actually *do something* it means diddly squat. Confidence comes from experience.

Practice Makes Confidence

The first time I ever wrote a feature I made a right pig's ear of it. My boss sat down with me and went through every single paragraph and showed me how to improve. At the time I had a real crisis of confidence as he detailed all the things I should have done but hadn't even thought of. I remember thinking, 'Oh *no*, I'll never be able to do this.' But I persevered (I had no choice – I would have lost my job otherwise) and the next feature was a bit better, the one after that better still. And now it never occurs to me to doubt it. I know that writing features is something I can do, ergo I'm confident about it.

Similarly, the first time I stood up in front of a group of people I was due to 'train' I was quaking in my high heels. But, despite my nerves, it went OK. No one seemed to question my right to be there, even if I was secretly asking myself *What am I doing here?* And what am *I* doing here? And 10 years later, although I might still get nervous sometimes when the stakes rise a little – like trying out a slightly different slant on the subject, or working with a group of people I suspect may be particularly taxing – I'm pretty confident I can do it. I can train. This is because my experience of training tells me I can do it. If I'd ducked out and hadn't tried it that first time, I'm sure I wouldn't be doing it now. And I would have missed out on something I love doing and which provides me with a good livelihood.

It's not only Mike Maynard and I who believe practice makes confident. Here are some quotes from people from all walks of life (and pages of history):

With every risk you take, you become stronger, wiser, more confident.
Mandi Norwood, former *Cosmopolitan* editor – now editor of *Mademoiselle* in New York

I felt I was in the doldrums, then I heard this guy called Geoff Thompson talking on the radio about his life as a nightclub bouncer (he was publicizing his book, *Watch My Back*). He said physical violence had never been part of his life and he overcame his fear of it by putting himself in the most violent situation he could think of to deal with it. I was impressed by his idea of looking at your fears and starting to systematically tackle them one by one, from small fears first, building up to bigger fears. And so I started addressing my fears, starting with the little ones like asking people who owed me money for that money, to taking risks about work; moving on to the higher-level ones like confronting a fear of physical violence. For that I plan to go to a kickboxing class.

How did I do that? I more or less just got on and did them. Having the concept that this was a very usual thing and would help my personal development helped me to face up to these things. They've all felt OK so far, giving me a sense of power. Life has become a lot easier because things I've put off for long time I'm actually doing. And afterwards I have an enormous sense of self-fulfilment.
Bob Griffiths, life coach

The only way to get rid of the fear of doing something is to go out and do it.
Susan Jeffers, author of *Feel the Fear and Do It Anyway*

I don't think it's possible to train yourself to do everything or achieve everything or be everything. Sometimes you can work very hard and it still won't happen. But I do think that confidence requires work. If you're not lucky enough to have confidence drummed into you by parents who didn't put a foot wrong, what you tend to do during your late teens and twenties is start re-building confidence. That does require a lot of discipline, but you can do it.
Anna Maxted, novelist

If you have aspirations to do something, always have a go at achieving it.
Jo-Ellen Gryzb, career specialist

You just do the thing you think you cannot do.
Eleanor Roosevelt, former first lady

Dr David McClelland, a leading authority on achievement motivation, summarized years of research on self-confidence by saying that the most important factor for developing self-confidence is to *master the needed skills*. Your mother, your friends and your teachers may tell you that you are not good at a task X. However, if you know *how* to X well enough, you can feel confident about X no matter what they think. Likewise, if everyone else tells you are great at Y, but you know that you *don't know how* to do Y well enough, you will lack confidence.

☆ Star Tip

We can improve our skills through watching and learning from others who are experts, reading, taking classes, but most of all from *practice*. Dr David McClelland said *the more we immerse ourselves in learning the skill, the faster we will learn.*

Having said all this, don't go mad. The key to building your confidence via actions, via achieving goals, is to make your goals just the right size. Not too big, so you scare yourself silly, not so small that you diss – or dismiss – them to yourself. But, like Goldilocks with Baby Bear's porridge, you pick the ones that are just right for you.

The easier the task, the more confidence you will feel that you can perform well; the harder it is, the less courage you will have. If your expectations and goals are too high, it will cause you to feel less confidence and more self-doubt. Then you run the risk you won't do it and disappoint yourself.

Sometimes, it's true, you have to take a leap, take a risk and do something big. It's hard to break certain actions down into smaller parts – like, say, going to college. But, wherever possible, you need to take *baby steps*.

A very successful American football coach, Vince Lombardy, who became famous for 'making winners of losers', suggested that no matter how 'bad' we are, we start with simple, small goals and do our best in order to 'get in the habit of winning'. This way we get a 'winning feeling' and a 'winning expectation'. He used to get his team to try their best to win even the practice pre-season games to get this 'winning feeling' going. And it worked.

Know that, whatever happens, you'll handle it, and whatever happens, you'll learn from it. If you can adjust your attitude to regard whatever it is you choose to try out as a learning experience, it takes the charge out of perfectionist, all-or-nothing thinking.

How This Fits with Our Case History

Remember Margaret and her difficult discussion with her difficult deputy?

Once she'd had coaching and role-played it in our training session, there still came a time when she had to actually do it. She had to sit down with her deputy and have that difficult conversation.

As it was, it went well and she felt good.

This is what she said afterwards:

This might sound like just one small step for me but it felt like a huge leap. I had crossed a line I had never crossed before. Next time it would be easier. Although this experience made me feel very proud of myself, I know similar situations will arise in the future and that each one will need to be tackled with conscious thought about my wording and behaviour. Then, hopefully, after much practice, asserting myself will come naturally. But for now, I feel like a huge burden has been lifted from me. I feel I have gained control again. I feel a million times more confident.

How to Set Your Own Goals

One psychological survey which asked 3,000 people 'What do you have to live for?' found that 90 per cent were simply enduring the present and waiting for something to happen. These people did not have goals.

OK, let's be businesslike about this. In business, there's an easy mnemonic for goal-setting which is useful in every area of life.

This is the art of setting SMART goals.

> **S stands for *specific*.** Vague goals like 'I must lose weight' do not work; specific goals like 'I will lose one pound a week for the next eight weeks' do.
>
> **M stands for *measurable*.** Not every goal is measurable (you can't judge *exactly* how much your self-esteem has improved, for example). But many goals are, and the more measurable the better. The above weight-loss goal is admirably measurable. A similar measurable goal might be 'I'll improve my relationship by having a "date" like we used to have once a week.' You measure it by simply noticing if the weekly date has happened.
>
> **A and R stand for *achievable* and *realistic*.** No point aiming to be a millionaire by next Wednesday when you're currently working in Woolworths. Breaking big goals down into smaller, attainable chunks is the way to get successful.
>
> **T stands for *timed*.** That is, you set a deadline, a time to review your goal. This means formulating a plan of action with a deadline: 'I will tackle my boss about a rise by this date next month' or 'I will go on three blind dates in the next three months.'

At 26, Miranda was wondering why she never seemed to meet any men with romantic possibilities. Then, she says, 'I realized all my male friends were gay, I was hanging out with gay people all the time. So I set myself a goal of meeting lots of straight men over the next six months. I planned it like a military campaign, having decided that, in that period, I'd do all I could to meet straight men – ask my friends, go to parties, join a gym. It worked. Within three months I'd met a lovely man and I'm still with him two years later.'

Put It All into Practice

Now you have your goals it's time to set about achieving them.
And, yes, this will require changing your behaviour — and change
is always stressful. Big change feels bigtime stressful, but even
little changes feel weird until you get used to them. So, seriously
think about how you'll look after yourself while you're going
about your goals.

Some Things That Help

Stick reminders of your goals around the house, in your car, in
your diary; tell a friend about your goals so she can be your 'goals
buddy' (maybe your friend sets her own goals and you buddy
each other), tell people about your goals *as if they're already
happening.* When I was a magazine editor, my then-deputy stood
up in front of all the staff at a magazine conference and
announced she was going to be an editor by the age of 25. She
was 24 at the time. There was a sharp intake of breath from the
rest of the staff, but she achieved her dream, then started setting
bigger goals. This year she achieved a lifelong dream of becoming
an editor in New York.

Set a time each week to review your progress. As long as you're
doing all these things, magic will start to happen.

Exercise

What Am I Going to Try?

You could go back to the list you made at the end of Chapter 3. Or you could create goals from the information you gained by doing the Confidence Grid at the end of Chapter 1. Or you can make a list now of goals you would like to tackle in order to build your confidence.

Choose five areas where you'd like to try something different which would increase your confidence. Don't forget to make those goals SMART.

For example, confident dreams like these:

▶ 'I'd like to stand on my own two feet with my family more'
▶ 'I'd like to not always feel like I'm the dogsbody at work'
▶ 'I'd like to lose weight'
▶ 'I'd like to get a boyfriend'
▶ 'I'd like to spend more time with people I really have fun with and care about' ...

can be turned into goals like these:

▶ 'By the end of November I am going to tell my parents I don't want to spend Christmas with them this year.'
▶ 'The next time my manager at work delegates three things to me at once I'm going to tell him I can only do two of them.'

▶ 'By the end of the month I'm going to join a gym to get fit.'

▶ 'By six month's time I'd like to have gone on three blind dates.'

▶ 'By the end of next week I'll have told Sally I'm not going to go to the pub every Tuesday night anymore.'

Then you create baby steps which will get you there:

▶ I'll call my sister and get her support in my decision.

▶ I'll practise saying no with my best friend role-playing my manager.

▶ I'll call three local gyms and find out about prices.

▶ I'll mention my plan to my best friend/sister and find out if she has any single male friends who might be interested in a blind date.

▶ I'll practise in front of the mirror telling Sally what I want to say, having defined my purpose and come up with a core statement.

My Dreams

1 _____

2 _____

3 _____

4 _____

5 _____

My Goals

1 _____

2 _____

3 _____

4 _____

5 _____

The Baby Steps I'm Going to Take to Get There

1 _____

2 _____

3 _____

4 _____

5 _____

Now choose one.

✑ Action Contract

I, _____, commit to doing

_____ by _____.

Whatever happens, I'll handle it. Whatever happens, I'll learn from it. And whatever happens, I'll try my best to enjoy it. And, whatever happens, I promise not to criticize myself for it.

Signed, _____

Then, as the ads say, just do it! Good luck.

Tools for Getting Yourself through It

▶   Affirmations/positive self-talk. The key is to encourage yourself before, during and after the 'action' you've chosen, making statements like, 'I know I can do this.'
▶   Visualization. See yourself doing it.
▶   Using Rescue Remedy, available from health food shops and chemists, including Boots
▶   Support – talking to friends, letting them know what you're doing
▶   Deep breathing
▶   Information
▶   Looking the part
▶   Standing up straight
▶   Taking your time – speaking slowly

☆ Star Tip

Organize your space, organize your life.

Mess creates a messy mind. Equally, minds become messy when there's mess around. Knowing you can tackle the mess helps set you up to know you can tackle anything. Every little change you make, every little challenge you rise to, is teaching you you *can* tackle challenge, you *can* make changes. And that sets you on the road to feeling confident you can tackle anything life throws at you.

11

Doing the Knowledge

I was new to the job of magazine editor, having decided to make a career change from marketing, but despite being so 'green' I had very little training at my new company. So I just got stuck in, picking up what guidance I could at every opportunity and doing what I thought was right. I talked to people outside the company, I asked colleagues lots of questions to try to find answers. I read as much as I could about the field, and I tried to keep an eye on what other magazines were doing.

But despite all that, I always had a horrible nagging feeling that either I wasn't doing the job right, or that there were a million better ways to do it that I was blissfully unaware of. I constantly carried this feeling around that I was going to get 'found out' one day, and that I would be 'exposed', because I'd never been formally trained for the job, and was nothing but a sham!

Then I finally persuaded my boss to let me go on a professional magazine editors' training course in London. I learned a lot in the two days, and it was a really excellent experience, but there was an unexpected spin-off from it. I came away feeling so much more confident.

I realized during the course that much of what I had been doing through instinct was, in fact, right, and that there weren't rafts of amazing secrets about the work that everyone else was using and that I didn't know about. I still have an enormous amount to learn, of course, but I realized I was on the right track, which was a wonderful discovery!

I went back to my desk with a much more confident approach to my work. It was great to have someone whose experience I respected telling me that I was doing OK. I'm still benefiting from it now, and it has given me the courage to go out and chase other challenges, because I know now that my 'sense' for the job is right. It was a very valuable experience, and those two days have made a big difference to the way I feel both about myself in my job, and how I can now tackle the future.

Lucy, magazine editor, on the importance of knowing what you're doing

One definition of confidence is knowing you have the right motivation, knowledge and skills to reach your goals. *Knowledge* is a crucial word here. Remember how right at the beginning of this book I said we are confident about things we *know* we can do?

Sometimes when we lack confidence we simply lack the right information, as did Lucy whose story begins this chapter. Sometimes when we lack confidence we wilfully prevent ourselves having the knowledge, and that keeps us stuck in an insecure and fearful place.

Jane was a chronically unconfident person. She didn't take her A levels because she was sure she'd fail them; she drifted into a dead-end job that was way below her potential skills and intelligence because she didn't believe she could do any better. But gradually, over the course of around five years, she realized she could do more and decided to re-take her A levels at night school. But even though Jane turned up for the classes and enjoyed the subjects, when the time came to take the exams she found herself repeating what she'd done at school and just didn't revise. Unsurprisingly, she failed.

But her class teacher knew how bright Jane was, took her aside and had a word. Jane says, 'He said to me he knew I was bright and he reckoned I'd not worked because I wasn't confident about passing the exam. He said that if *I* wasn't confident, he was and he knew I could pass if only I did the work. He said I was my own worst enemy and my lack of confidence was the only thing holding me back. And what he said did move me. I was shocked to hear it come from someone else. I thought about it and I went to class again and I worked this time and took my exams and passed them – my grades were an A, a B and a C. Not bad at all!'

Recently Jane started working as a primary school teacher and is happier than she's been in years.

So – whatever your situation, don't sabotage yourself via inadequate preparation.

Ask yourself: Do I have all the knowledge I need for this situation? Have I done the work? The preparation?

If it's a job interview, ask yourself: Have I read up about the company? When I was hiring writers to work on *Cosmopolitan* I wouldn't consider anyone who hadn't had a thorough read of the magazine and boned up on the various sections within it. It was amazing how many hadn't bothered!

Some things – like a date, for instance – are hard to prepare for. If you're going to see a movie you could always read a couple of film reviews if you're nervous you'll say something silly. One well-known magazine editor confessed recently she goes to see the film *before* the date so she can form an opinion on it before the date. I'd say that was going too far – but does illustrate the extent to which some people will take the Boy Scout motto 'Be Prepared'!

We can sabotage ourselves by not preparing, by not doing the work. And that only keeps us unconfident.

Exercise

What can you do to prepare yourself for your chosen task? If it's tackling a relationships matter you can read other self-help books which deal with relationship issues. If it's to do with work, taking a course or passing an exam, you can read as much and as extensively as you can. Or search the net. You could straw-poll friends and colleagues, asking them what they think. Even if it's a date you can read the papers and think of things to talk about or ask friends what *they* talk about on dates if you're out of practice.

- ▶ List important areas where you don't feel as confident or skilled as you would like for success and happiness in your career, relationships, or personal life.
- ▶ For each area, list potential learning opportunities – books, classes, counselling, workshops, observing people who can serve as 'models', practice, or use feedback or other life experiences that can help you develop your skills.
- ▶ Develop definite goals and plans for improving skills. Build them into your personal goals list.

See It and Believe It

Every moment of your life is infinitely creative and the universe is endlessly bountiful. Just put forth a clear enough request, and everything your heart desires will come to you.
Shakti Gawain, visualization guru and author of *Creative Visualization*

If you want something bad enough, the whole earth conspires to help you get it.
Madonna, pop phenomenon and the queen of getting what she wants

Beware! Here is a powerful tool which will help you increase your confidence, without having to move off the sofa.

Again, it might sound silly to you, but it's used by top international sports coaches, by celebrities and movie stars and thousands of not-so famous people who have found it helped them to get to the top of their own worlds. It's visualization. Literally, creating a mental image of what you want to achieve, how you want to be. It works like magic – although there's plenty of science to back it up and prove it isn't straight out of Harry Potter. Whatever it is, it *is* effective.

I came across this technique when I was ill in the early 1990s with Chronic Fatigue Syndrome. At that time, and with that condition, I didn't have many action-oriented options open to me, and there wasn't anything conventional medicine could do. I felt despairing, especially after a doctor told me there was nothing they could do 'and all I can guarantee you is you'll be very mis-erable for at least six months.' I felt angry at being told how I'd feel for such a long time (and that it wouldn't be good) and I thought, 'I'll try anything to prove him wrong, and this at any rate can't do any harm.'

So I started to visualize myself running about bursting with energy. The illness gave me a dispiriting variety of food allergies and there were many things I couldn't eat. So one of my favourite images I held in my mind was of my partner and I sitting in a square in Italy eating pizza and drinking champagne (both things made me horribly ill at the time).

I held these images in my mind, combining them with affirmations about being totally well. On bad days, when I wondered if I'd ever get better, being able to access these images – and the promise that they would help – really did help. And it worked. I got better. It didn't happen overnight, but I did eventually fully recover from Chronic Fatigue Syndrome, which was lucky because not all Chronic Fatigue sufferers make a full recovery. OK, I lost the partner. (C'est la vie!) But now I can run about to my heart's content and eat pizza and drink the occasional glass of bubbly with whomever I choose.

And I'm not the only one who has benefited from visualization.

One renowned psychologist says, 'A college student in one of my classes was an Olympic marksman. In the past he had been prac- tising daily; but now he no longer had time to practise daily, because the practice site was so far away. Instead, he learned to use mental imagery to practise. Six times a week, he imagined – in great detail – shooting at targets as if he were at the target range. Once a week he shot at the range. His shooting scores continued to rise *at the same rate* as when he had practised seven days a week shooting real bullets at the real target range.'

Spoookee. But also proof visualization works.

In a controlled experiment, students in Australia who had never shot a basketball used mental imagery to learn how to shoot bas- kets. During later tests, those using imagery shot as accurately as students who practised shooting real basketballs. In other con- trolled experiments, people learned to increase communication skills by mental role-playing.

If you're struggling with believing, say, you could be confident, or successful, or happy, or even slim, it might be that you literally cannot imagine it. Perhaps that's because you've not actually tried getting a clear mental image of either doing a task successfully or feeling confident. Well, now you can start. And thankfully it's easy.

Visualizing Success

Remember we talked about how negative beliefs about ourselves create negative self-fulfilling prophecies? Visualizing our success is a way to break that cycle and replace it with a positive self-fulfilling prophecy. In your mind's eye, see yourself being successful in whatever it is you are choosing to do. See yourself standing tall, breathing deeply, looking relaxed. See yourself smiling, looking confident. Get a sense of how this might feel. Take yourself through a little scenario which has you as the heroine of your own movie script. For example, for a job interview: 'I am walking into the room, the interviewers look up and like the look of me, I smile confidently, I am feeling good. They motion me to sit down and I walk slowly and carefully to the seat and sit down comfortably. They ask me an opening question and I think, "This is OK, this is easy" and I answer confidently, speaking slowly, making eye contact and smiling ...' and so on.

Always give it a successful outcome: 'I see myself leaving the room thinking, "That went really well." I see the job offer coming through my letterbox and landing on the doormat. I open it and I am ecstatic. I know I can do the job.'

You can use this formula for any situation: a date, a difficult conversation with your sister, a big work presentation. When you've done it the once, keep it in mind and re-run it every time you feel nervous. It helps. Another tool in your confident tool box.

Exercise

Beware What You Ask for – These Work!

▶   Draw a picture and put it somewhere. You might have
    fun with it and do a collage of your head on a picture
    of a confident body in a business meeting – if that's
    what you want.

▶   Sit down quietly, close your eyes and create a
    visualization as a meditation. Imagine a mental movie
    screen in your mind's eye and run your scenario
    there.

▶   Authoring your own success: Write out what you
    want to see in the present tense. For example: 'I get
    up, the sun is shining, I take a deep breath and look
    forward to the day ahead. Yes, this day has a big
    important meeting in it, but I feel confident I can get
    through it and perform well. I go to the bathroom and
    brush my teeth and as I look at myself in the mirror,
    I tell myself: "You can do this. You're looking good
    today." I get dressed, putting on clothes that make me
    feel good as well as look good. I leave the house with
    plenty of time to get to my meeting so I'll be relaxed
    when I arrive. The train arrives bang on time ...'

You get the idea.

☆ **Star Tip**
    Bring your image to mind just as you fall asleep. This helps
    the visualization sink deep into your unconscious mind
    and speeds up the process of making feeling and behaving
    differently a confident reality.

Emotional Rescue

This section is about how to manage the fear that appears when we do something different, when we stretch ourselves, when we take on new challenges.

Strong emotions like fear can sabotage our best efforts. It really is a case of, to quote that book again, feeling the fear and doing it anyway.

Fear

Fear will appear around any situation you feel wobbly about. One effective technique is to chase the fear through to its ultimate conclusion. This is a mental/emotional technique recommended in the scared-person's bible, *Feel the Fear and Do It Anyway*. You think: what's the worst thing that can possibly happen? If it's something like, 'I'll run out of things to say and just sit there silent in this interview and I won't get the job,' you then think, 'And then what will happen? I sit there silent. So what?' Very rarely, if ever, is the answer likely to be: 'And then I might die.' No one has ever died of a job interview, have they? Remember what Susan Jeffers, author of *Feel the Fear . . .*, recommends – reminding yourself 'Whatever happens, I'll handle it.'

For fear on the day, try Rescue Remedy, available from most chemists. A few drops on the tongue really do calm you down before a gruelling situation. Try it.

Most important: Breathe!

Use anti-fear affirmations:

▶   'I am in control of my fear.'
▶   'I am confident.'
▶   'This may be difficult but it's not impossible.'
▶   'I can do this.'
▶   'Whatever happens, I'll handle it.'

Before the event, sit and feel that fear. Notice where it is in your body. Fighting it makes things worse. Just sitting and acknowledging it means it's not running you while you try to run away from it.

Call a friend and tell them how you're feeling and that you need them to say something encouraging. Then listen – and believe!

The night before a taxing challenge, watch a comedy video. It will take your mind off your fears, and laughing will relax you.

Anchoring

This is an exercise from neuro-linguistic programming which can help.

Step One   (Before you feel afraid): remember a time in your life when you felt totally calm and totally relaxed. Sit quietly and bring that occasion to mind. Really let it sink in, the feelings, the sensations, the sounds. See yourself bright and full of colour. Feel the confidence and the calm.

Step Two   When you really feel the rush of good feeling, press two of your fingers together – this is the 'anchor'. Shake yourself out and repeat the experience. Every time you reach the peak of good feeling, 'anchor' those fingers together again.

Practise this until pushing those fingers together gives you the good feeling.

Step Three   Whenever you feel afraid, doubtful, nervous, 'anchor' those two fingers together and access the good feeling which you have now associated with that movement.

12

Intuition

Your Confident Friend

One thing I've learned that has improved my confidence no end, and that's the truth of my intuition. When I was younger, I was forever ignoring my gut instincts and going with what I thought was right, or what other people told me I should do. I ignored my instincts about men, about friends, about work, and finally I said yes to a job which I knew really I shouldn't take on and which I didn't think I'd like because my husband thought it was a good idea. And I got ill. Very ill. And lying in bed I thought, 'I *knew* I shouldn't have done this.' After that I started to listen to my instincts more, because not listening had actually got me ill. I started to trust them, to follow them and act on them. And they've never let me down. And that helps me be more confident – because I have this inner barometer for making right choices.
Sandra, 35

Intuition is not a fake. It really works. We all have it. We can all hear it. Many of us ignore it, but in my experience it's always right. And intuition is a powerful resource for confidence – once you know you can trust it, your confidence in yourself increases no end.

Its messages may come in many forms: a bad feeling ('this just doesn't feel right'), a lack of enthusiasm for something which, on the surface, looks great, a huge boost of energy when you hit on something that's right, an 'aha' moment when you hear a fabulous idea, even a nagging doubt …

I haven't always trusted mine. Like Sandra, I too took on a job I didn't really want and it was a disaster. There was another time when I had started dating a lovely-looking, lovely-seeming man. I had a dream of him sitting in a chair, with a little door where his heart should be, casually flicking knives at me from a small cupboard behind the door. Six months down the line, guess what? I discovered he was a casual heartbreaker.

That was a very vivid example of intuition in action. Unfortunately its messages don't always arrive this plainly (even so, I ignored it and dated him for six months. But the experience of remembering the dream and realizing its accuracy made me more confident about any strange dreams I might have in the future).

But intuition is like any other muscle: exercise it, trust it, and it kicks in even stronger.

It helps to know the form your own intuition takes. Think of past times when you said 'I *knew* it!' and think: *what* did you know? How did the information come to you? Via feelings, thoughts, actions? Was it located somewhere in your body – a sinking feeling in the stomach, an increase in heart rate, an all-over tingle? Did it come in dreams? Did it operate mentally as a flashing insight? Or a nagging 'Yes, *but*'? Or arrive emotionally as an 'irrational' fear? A flash of anger?

Follow your instincts, that's where true wisdom manifests itself.
Oprah Winfrey

Your gut reaction is the right one.
Lucie Jackson, 23, stockbroker

Once you know how your intuition works for you, you can be confident of any decision, any action you base on it. Trusting yourself, knowing you can trust yourself, improves your confidence enormously.

Affirmations for increasing your intuition:

> 'I can trust my intuition.'
> 'I now choose to listen to my inner voice.'
> 'By trusting my intuition my confidence expands.'
> 'Knowing I can trust myself makes me feel confident.'

Exercise

Ponder these questions:

When in my life has my intuition been right, whether I followed it or not?

How did my intuition show itself to me (a feeling, a nagging doubt, etc.)?

Is there anything my intuition keeps telling me now which I keep ignoring?

Making a Confident Decision

I have always found decision-making really difficult. In my last job, instant decisions were demanded of me all the time and I found it incredibly stressful. I could often see the advantage of lots of different options and I lacked the confidence to go with any single one. So I used to procrastinate. 'Let me think about it' was my watchword. But then I wouldn't think about it, because thinking about it reminded me how terrifying the thought of deciding – and getting it wrong – was. It got so I nearly lost my job because of it and I realized I had to change. About the same time I had some coaching and I was encouraged to just experiment with deciding. So I started sometimes just choosing something, anything, even though I wasn't sure. And sometimes it worked and sometimes it didn't. But, the interesting thing was, I found the anxiety went away once I'd decided. And I learned that, even if I made the wrong decision, the world didn't end. And people seemed to respect me more for making even a wrong decision than no decision at all.

Amanda, 31, formerly indecisive marketing executive

Given anxiety is the plague of the unconfident person, making a decision can send you into a tailspin. Procrastination is the haven of the underconfident. If you put things off, you don't have to deal with the decision.

So you do put things off, or you avoid putting yourself in situations where you have to decide. Decisions often lead to a lot of other horribles you don't want to contemplate because you lack confidence about them: things like responsibility (it was my decision, so I'm responsible for it), and action (if I decide, then I'll have to do something about it).

Alternatively, you may not be procrastinating but prevaricating. You'd be perfectly willing to act, if only you knew which action you wanted to take or was required.

Life is awash with decisions. Big decisions – should I marry this person? Should I take this job? Should I re-train as a barrister? And little decisions – should I go out tonight when I feel I'm getting a cold? Should I choose the chilli or the pizza?

But if you keep putting them off, you just stack up a sackful of 'unfinished business'. Which is the mental equivalent of never throwing anything away, and leaves your psyche full of clutter. And that only racks up stress. Having a to-do list that looks like *War and Peace* is stressful. You start avoiding a friend because you haven't decided whether or not to go on holiday with her; you avoid answering the phone because you haven't decided whether or not to date that semi-cute man you met last week; you become wracked with jealousy when a colleague lands a promotion you hadn't decided whether to go for or not. And so on.

There must be a better way, right? And there is. Tackling those decisions. Arming yourself with decision-making tools to help you.

For all our social skills, we're seldom taught how to make decisions, how to weigh up options. Our parents tell us what to do and we do it. Or our parents never act decisively for themselves, giving us the message that deciding is somehow difficult or wrong.

But really, decisions aren't that bad. And practising making them helps us feel – hallelujah – more confident.

As I said earlier, my thing used to be obsessing over the 'right' thing. And in the end I came to the conclusion that there is no 'right' thing – only the right thing for me at the time. Plus, as I discovered when I left my second husband, sometimes what the world might view as the 'wrong' thing is the right thing after all.

Often, thinking it through gets us nowhere. Mainly because we get caught up in our blind alleys – our fear of failure, our negative beliefs. Here are some alternatives to sleepless nights that I hope will help:

Decision-making Strategies for Ordinary, Everyday Decisions

NB Use your self-awareness here. What does go on when you need to decide? If you're a habitual procrastinator, then asking for more time is not really what you need. If, however, you're a knee-jerk yes-woman, then asking for time would be a good idea.

▶ Just decide! Pizza or chilli. Choose one. Practising making small decisions instantly helps with making slightly bigger decisions.

▶ Go with your gut instinct (see Intuition, above).

▶ If in doubt, say no.

▶ Ask yourself: Do I have enough information? Asking for more input sometimes makes things clearer.

▶ Give yourself time (*NB habitual procrastinators can ignore this one!*)

▶ It's OK to say 'I don't know.'

▶ In some circumstances, it helps to ask the person asking the question what *they* think. In my experience, this works better at work. If, for example, the question is something like, 'Shall we go with the red packaging or the blue?' asking around for the majority opinion can be valuable. If, however, your mother is pressurizing you to come home for Christmas, there's no point asking for her opinion because *of course* she's going to say come.

▶ Remember the third way. Often we're faced with
   either/or decisions – do this or that. Ask yourself, is
   there another option, a better way? When we're
   stressed we're especially prone to this tunnel-thinking.
   Like a tunnel vision of the mind.

Remember, even after you've decided you have the right to
change your mind.

Second thing to remember: you don't have to justify your decision.
Often we know what we really want but don't want to say so for
fear of hurting someone or incurring their disapproval, so then
we face another decision: how to justify our original decision.
Remember what we said about clear, assertive communication.
Just make your statement and stick with it. If they ask for reasons,
fine. Often people don't. They just want the decision, simple as
that.

☆ **Star Tip**

Be very suspicious of those 'should' and 'ought' voices in
your head. Do not make any decisions based on what you
'should' do. As in, 'I should stay with this person' (when a
little voice tells you you'd be better off leaving).

Decision-making Strategies for Big, Possibly Life-changing Decisions

Here's a powerful technique for accessing your inner knowing
which allows intuition to show itself:

▶ Suppose you've been offered a new job which you're
   unsure about. Sit quietly, eyes shut, and imagine it's six
   months' hence and you're there, doing that job. Really

feel your way into it. Sense the sounds, the smells, feel yourself into the tasks you'd be doing. Keep this up for a couple of minutes and notice the thoughts, feelings, impressions that come up.

► Now imagine yourself six months' hence having turned the job down. See yourself still in your current job, and again notice your thoughts, feelings, impressions.

What you're looking for is a sense of relief, or excitement, about either option which will be an inner indication far more valuable than hours of analysing.

I did this in 1995 when I was deciding whether to take the job of deputy editor at *Cosmopolitan*. When I imagined doing it, I felt excited. When I imagined not doing it, I felt jealous of whoever was. That was information enough for me.

► Talk the various options out and see how you feel about them. You don't have to struggle all on your own with these things. Ask friends if they're willing to hear you out. Women, especially, often talk in order to see how they feel about things (men, on the other hand, tend to think things through alone, then talk once they've made a decision).
NB This is not the same as asking friends for advice. Let them know that. Yes, they will probably have an opinion about what you should do, but people who lack confidence tend to spend too much time asking for advice and too little time trusting their own impulses.

► Make a list of the pros and cons. List the pros and cons of both sides of the decision. So, if I decide this

way, these good things and these bad things might be
the consequences; and if I decide the other way, these
good things and these bad things may be the consequences. This is a favourite technique of thinkers –
people who operate primarily from their heads.
But often when a thinker makes a list, they get a
non-thought reaction. You notice you're weighting one
side with negatives because, yes, you do really want to
do the other thing. Or you notice that, although this
one only has one 'con', it's a huge con and it doesn't
feel right.

From the Sublime to the Ridiculous

This is a technique from life-coaching which I've found useful. Get
a piece of paper and write 'sublime' at the top of the left-hand
side and 'ridiculous' at the top right. Now place your options as
they fall in a V shape on the page. For example, say you harbour
a secret desire to be a sculptor. Under 'sublime' you might write
'Take three years off and go to art college.' Under ridiculous, you
might write 'Call up Richard Branson and see if he'd like me to
make a plastic cow for his back garden.' In the middle you write
relatively sensible, achievable options, like 'Go to an evening class
and start making things.' This exercise, with its ridiculous element,
helps you make creative options you might not have thought of
(often, even workable options seem ridiculous at first). The trick
lies in making yourself sit there and for long enough and not give
up. It's then that the right side of your brain kicks in and creative
options come into play.

It's good to do this with a friend. Often the most obvious options
don't occur to us because we tend, especially when anxious, to
operate tunnel-thinking.

☆ Star Tip

▶ Sometimes we can't make big decisions simply because we're not giving ourselves time to decide. We rush ourselves, or we dash about asking everyone else what they think. What we *don't* do is sit quietly with ourselves and say, 'OK what do *I* want?'

▶ Go for a walk and ponder it. Sit in the park and meditate on it. Ask the moon. Do whatever lights your candle, but give yourself *time*.

Q: What if I've done all this and I still don't know what I want?

I sympathize. It can be incredibly painful to not know what you want. If you've grown up with bossy parents who always told you what to do, or you've led a life characterized by extreme stress which always knocks people off-centre, or if you simply (although who says it's simple?) chronically lack confidence, you may, under all the terror, genuinely not know what you want.

Don't despair.

Things to try:

▶ Affirm: 'The more I get to know myself, the more I know what I want.'

▶ Try keeping a journal. Writing down your thoughts and feelings every day can be a very powerful tool in getting to know yourself better. Often you read back over what you've written and think, 'Yes, I really do want so-and-so, so what's holding me back?'

▶ Counselling/therapy. Or life-coaching. Not all therapy needs to take ages and cost a fortune.

NB Bear in mind that any kind of addiction can dull our feeling and take us away from ourselves. If you're drinking too much, taking too many drugs or indulging in any kind of addictive behaviour (even addiction to romance!) it can act as a major distraction from knowing what you really want out of life. Deciding to tackle any kind of addiction is a positive step in decision-making! Also, when we're stressed, running around like headless chickens and not thinking straight, we won't know if we're coming or going. Stop. Take a break. Go on holiday. Spend some time alone. It is very difficult to tune out all those voices telling us what to do.

Finally, one option is to live with not knowing. And hold the intention that you want to find out.

☆ Star Tip

Reward yourself for deciding. Don't instantly start putting yourself down, as in 'God, I really made a meal out of that one.' Try telling yourself, 'I did really well there. It was a difficult decision for me and I made it.' I know this feels stupid at first, but it's the only way.

Finally:

Remember the mantra: **'Whatever happens, I'll handle it.'**

13

Finding Your Confident Part

> Even on a bad day, I can put bad feelings aside and roll-on
> my confident part. Then, when I've finished what I needed to
> be confident for – training, for example – I can go home and go
> to pieces.
> **Me!**

Remember in Part One we talked about your unconfident part
– the part that is terrified? Well, she's about to meet her nemesis – your confident part.

All confident (seeming) people have a role they put on, an act
they go into, a confident mask they can hide behind when they
need to appear super-confident, even when part of them is
quietly having kittens.

To access your own confident part, think about those times when
you can be confident. Are there any confidence tricks you use
already? Is there a 'persona' you put on or go into? Which situations are you most confident in? What does that feel like inside?

If you don't have a confident part inside, you're going to have to
create one! And you can have fun cultivating an inner personality
who fears nothing and no one.

Exercise

Create Your Confident Part

You could draw your confident part and pin her on the wall.
Write her down. Go through some magazines and rip out a
picture of someone looking confident to give you inspiration.

If this leaves you blank, what about a confident role model?

Who might your confident role model be, and why?

Some suggestions:

> Madonna (the queen of confidence)
> Princess Diana (even though we know she was
> insecure underneath, she could smile and let the
> vulnerability shine through. And people loved her)
> Mo Mowlem (driven, determined, I'll do it anyway)
> any of the Spice Girls (confident girl power)
> Margaret Thatcher (God forbid, but she did have
> confidence)
> Audrey Hepburn (cheeky, smily, elegant)
> Marilyn Monroe (sex on a stick, with a wiggle)
> Lauren Bacall (the epitome of cool)
> Naomi Campbell, Claudia Schiffer, Kate Moss or
> indeed any supermodel (confident walk, confident
> smile, the-whole-world-adores-me attitude – but not
> the super-skinniness, please!)
> Zoe Ball (the cheekiness to be yourself)
> Dawn French/Jennifer Saunders (make 'em laugh, make
> 'em like me, have a brain)

Think about whom you've chosen and how they might go about being confident in the situations which wobble you.

Or you might not choose a famous person but someone you know whom you'd like to be more like, a colleague or friend.

Observe them closely. Notice how they stand, smile, speak. Then, when you're going into your taxing situation where you need to feel confident, visualize them and know that you'll call on their qualities. Imagine yourself getting coaching from them. Have fun with this: if you can make yourself laugh, so much the better.

Confidence Buddies

It's hard doing this confidence-building work all on your own. Sometimes you will wobble. Sometimes you'll feel down and like it's never going to happen. Sometimes you need help, and support, or a shoulder to cry on.

That's when you need your network.

Your confidence will grow far more abundantly if you have some-one watering your garden, fertilizing your soil and helping you push yourself up through the earth. But you need also to hand-pick this person carefully. Choose the wrong person – someone who might slay you with an ill-timed remark, or treat you as though your confidence doesn't matter – and it could all go horribly wrong.

And we don't want that, you and I.

The confident key is to *spend more time with people who help you feel better about yourself, and less time with those who don't.*

You might choose one person who will know what you're going through – someone you can phone when you're tackling a challenge and let them know so they can help you coach yourself through it by prompting you if you have temporarily forgotten how. You might choose another shy person and you can encourage each other. Or you might choose someone you already see as confident, so they can give you a few tips while they're about it.

Either way, choose someone with a big heart.

Don't choose anyone …

► who has ever criticized you or put you down
► who is jealous of you, or doesn't have your best interests at heart
► who is always giving you advice, and doesn't like it if you don't take it.

You could choose a *mentor* – someone older and more experienced who is willing to listen, support and share with you what has worked and does work for them. This can help especially well around work matters – mentoring is more established in the workplace.

Exercise

1   Make a list of the friends who support you, and a list of those who don't. Make a decision not to share any of your confidence-building processes with the second lot – this is a vulnerable area and you need to protect it.

2   Now choose someone from the first list and call them – now. Ask them if they're willing to support you in

something you wish to tackle. If they say yes, tell them what you've chosen to tackle as your confidence-building goal and tell them how they can help you through it.

3   Bask in the good feelings this will bring about between you.

My supportive friends are: _____

My confidence buddy/ies is/are: _____

Your Confident Body Image

What matters most in life is to like and admire the person you see in the mirror.
Paula Bush, 21, student

Never eat more than you can lift.
Miss Piggy

The way we feel about our appearance is one of the biggest influences on our confidence. Feeling badly about how we look kills confidence quicker than Arnie Schwarzenegger with a big gun and a bad mood. Feeling good about how we look helps us feel we can tackle anything.

When I was younger I always had my hair too short for me and, while I secretly always wanted to go blonde, I couldn't muster up the confidence. When I finally did, at about age 34, it worked! It did feel good. It's kind of dark blonde now, not far off its natural colour. But the confidence hasn't gone away with the bottle blonde.

I also used to obsess about my weight. I don't anymore and, you know what? My weight is just the same. I eat more, but I'm fine. I accept my body now, even though it's giving in to gravity a little and probably doesn't look as good as when I didn't accept it.

Alcoholics Anonymous meetings begin with what members call the 'serenity prayer', which goes along the lines of: 'God, grant me the serenity to accept the things I cannot change, the courage to change the things I can, and the wisdom to know the difference.' This is a good mantra for dealing with your body image.

If you're telling yourself you're fat, or feeling fat, think about what you can do. 'I spent all my working hours thinking about how fat I was,' recalls sales assistant Amanda, 25. 'But instead of actually doing something about it, I kept stuffing my face with food and filling my head with thoughts of my size. Going to the gym made the difference. It took months before I began to feel better about my body, but I stopped having so many nasty, critical thoughts about my weight as soon as I made a proactive change.'

Excuse me while I roll out a cliché, but you only get one body in this life, so you might as well learn to love it. Think of all the energy you waste criticizing it. And criticizing it doesn't change it, it doesn't improve it. In fact, it makes it more likely you'll sabotage it by binge-eating to comfort yourself – when it was you made yourself feel bad in the first place.

What *can* you do?

►   Use affirmations to enhance your body image:
         'I love my body.'
         'I am learning to love and accept my body.'

'I approve of how I look.'
'I look good today.'

► Diet – not drastically, but steadily for real results.

► Exercise more – set a goal for your exercise regime and stick to it.

► Talk to your GP about seeing a counsellor about your binge-eating.

► Join a gym.

► Find a personal trainer.

► Try out that yoga class.

► Visit an image consultant.

► Or a colour clinic.

► Go blonde/red.

► Get your hair all cut off – or grow it. Ask your hairdresser what he/she thinks would suit your face.

► Go through your closets and throw out all those ratty outfits that don't make you feel good.

► Learn how to dress for your weight.

► Accentuate your good points – hands, nails, legs, cleavage.

► Learn how to make yourself up like a make-up artist.

► See your doctor about any medical problems that could be fixed (some thyroid problems make you overweight, some plastic surgery is available on the NHS, some skin problems can be cleared up with drugs).

► Try the Alexander Technique for chronic bad posture (for a list of practitioners in your area, write to The Society of Teachers of the Alexander Technique, 10 London House, 266 Fulham Road, London SW10 9EL).

Here are some uplifting thoughts for living with what you cannot change:

Don't try to be perfect. It's your little flaws that make you an attractive individual.
Sarah Heywood, 28, stylist

Sometimes a good feeling from inside is worth more than a beautician.
Mother Teresa

If God had meant women to worry about cellulite he wouldn't have put it where we can't see it.
Kate Murphy, 31, accountant

Finally ...

Remember how attractive any confident woman is – no matter what her size.

Audrey Hepburn once went to a Hollywood party populated with the curvy blondes who were all the rage when the petite brunette was also a star. Audrey didn't let this make her feel inadequate. Instead, she stood by a pillar and visualized herself as a slithery snake. Within minutes, most of the men in the room had gathered round Audrey. Such is the power of inner suggestion!

☆ **Star Tip**
Be extra careful at times when body image takes a battering. When you sleep with a man and he doesn't call. When you split up with a boyfriend. If someone criticizes your face or shape. After a bad haircut. Or a Christmas when you

inadvertently put on 11 pounds. When you find your first wrinkle. Or when your sister wins Miss World.

Exercise

The Budget Makeover

Get a friend to go through your wardrobe with you, suggesting combos you might not have tried; suggesting chuck-outs and things that just don't suit you. Get her to talk about makeup too, maybe ask her to make you up for a girly night in for a change.

Summary of Part Two: The Tools in Your Confidence Tool Kit

▶   You are aware of your body language and what confident messages look like.

▶   You have a selection of physical tricks (breathing, feeling your feet) to use to help you feel more confident.

▶   You say STOP to negative thoughts and talk to yourself like your own best friend.

▶   You *believe* in yourself as a confident person.

▶   You know how to sound confident and speak confidently – clearly, specifically.

▶   You are *au fait* with the techniques of adult communication.

▶   You have skills you can practise for dealing with conflict.

▶   You are willing and able to practise.

▶   You set small – and bigger – goals to practise confidence in real situations.

▶   You use visualization to help you.

▶   You have techniques for mastering fear.

▶   You trust your intuition to help you make decisions.

▶   You have a part of you which is confident and friends who support that part.

▶   You are learning to love your body and making the most of your appearance.

3

Applied
Confidence

14

Confidence Out There in the World

> If you want to become a barrister you don't just barge into court, there's some training to do. You can train yourself to be more confident but you've got to be disciplined about it. Once you've got the basic tools, you've just got to work hard.
>
> You can't jump out of bed every day bright, shiny and confident. There are some days when I think I'm writing this and who cares and it's rubbish and no one will ever want to read it. Confidence isn't a constant. It has its highs and lows, and that's natural. Otherwise you'd be an unbearable human being!
>
> **Anna Maxted, 30, novelist**

Now you have the tools, now have the knowledge, let's look at what you're going to do out there in the world and how you're going to do it.

This part of the book is all about putting everything we've looked at so far into practice in specific scary situations. We will look at how to be your own confidence coach in different areas of your life – relationships, work, dating. So you need never worry about anything ever again.

NB It's worth reading this whole section, given there are useful tips in all of it. For example, information about dealing with difficult people is in Chapter 15, while guidelines on tackling talking about difficult issues is in Chapter 18, and so on. Much of the material on relation-ships is relevant: whether you're talking about your lover, boss, family or friendships, the same guidelines apply.

Confident Relationships

I am confident at work, I know people see me as efficient there, and decisive. But when it comes to relationships I'm a quivering mess. I feel all at sea. I don't know what the rules are and even sticking to rules sometimes means things still foul up.

The longest relationship I've had was a year and that ended in disaster.

Work is so much easier. I do X and I can be pretty certain it will result in Y. But relationships are so much more complicated and unpredictable. You can never know what the other person's going to say, think or do. I guess that's what makes them excit-ing, but it's also what makes them so confusing and such bloody hard work.
Yasmina, 25

Agony aunts the world over would be down at their respective dole offices if relationships were a straightforward business. Relationships test our confidence in myriad ways. From whether we're brave enough to suggest a date to that cute guy in the sandwich shop who is *definitely* flirting (isn't he?) to whether we're confident enough to let a lover see our wobbly bits at full wobble. Whether we're confident enough to stand up to a father who's been bullying us for years, or find the courage to tell a sister we're not going to babysit her children for the sixth Saturday in a row. Whether we feel able to go alone to a party where we don't know *everyone* to whether we can muster up the front to break off seeing that oh-so-exhausting so-called 'friend'.

The payoffs of having the confidence to do all these things are as abundant as leaves on a tree. You get more time for yourself, you get more comfortable with yourself, you relax and you might even have fun. You might find your life changing in wonderful and unpredictable ways.

☆ Star Tip

*Don't try and change **THEM**.*

One thing you needn't be worrying about is whether you have the confidence to make other people change.

You Can Never Make Other People Change

You can only manage yourself, speak up for yourself, tell people what you don't like and what you want and see what happens. You can *ask* for change. But if they don't change, that's not your business. It's their business. And it's not your fault.

We often tie ourselves up in knots with mad thinking like 'If only I could have made him love me,' 'I should have made Mikey stop drinking,' 'I should have stopped her seeing Bruce.' Truth is, you couldn't have made those people do those things. People, including you, only do what they want to do, what they *can* do. You could, for example, have told Mikey you didn't like his drinking, which takes courage and confidence. You could have told your friend the reasons why you didn't like Bruce. But it would have been up to those individuals to decide what to do with the information. Chances are they'd have carried on regardless.

Your business is to manage yourself. But the magic of it is, often when we change ourselves, other people around us change and things do improve. But usually not in the ways we might have imagined.

Like Sarah, 31, who for years had run around doing everything for her super-critical mother, for whom nothing was ever good enough. Sarah would drop everything to go and see her mother when her mother called, even though it involved a long drive across London. She'd often turn up to find her mother had forgotten why she'd called, or to be subjected to a tirade about what a bad daughter she was and how she 'never' visited.

Being at her mother's beck and call in this way – and with such bitter rewards – was getting Sarah down and making her life a misery. Friends were complaining she was always cancelling them if her mother happened to need a loaf of bread; her partner was resentful. She says, 'One day I turned up and Mum threw the cake I'd bought her the week before at me. That put me at the end of my tether. I thought, "This can't go on." I was doing an assertiveness class at the time and I practised dealing with my mother and what I should say. I decided I'd only go there once a week at a specific time. I was nervous as hell about saying it, but I used broken record and just kept repeating "Mum, I've decided I'm going to come here once a week, on Tuesday evenings." She did kick up a stink. Called me a terrible daughter, which wasn't much different to what she called me normally anyhow. But a wonderful thing happened. She realized I meant it – and I've stuck to it. And she knows I'm her only child living in London, so if I don't go, no one goes, and now she accepts it. She no longer calls up demanding I go there at all hours. Really, all I wanted was to limit my time with her, I didn't imagine she'd start behaving herself. It's a miracle. And it feels so good that I made it happen.'

So, for Sarah, speaking up for herself, being clear about what she was willing to do and not do, did bring about (amazing) changes in her mother. Her mother had no choice but to go along with Sarah's rules once Sarah had laid them down. Before, she knew she could get away with anything.

☆ **Star Tip**

Knowing *you* can change things in a relationship brings a confidence that you can pull situations around.

Putting It All Together

To help her manage the super-charged relationship with her difficult mother, Sarah used all the confidence tricks in the book – that is, in *this* book:

▶ She defined her goal. Which was: only seeing her mother once a week, on Tuesdays. As goals go, it was Specific, Measurable, Achievable (hoorah!), certainly Relevant, and Timed. (It didn't have an end point – but was timed in that the time she'd see her mother was stated as Tuesdays.) – see page 110

▶ She communicated this clearly to her mother. – page 81

▶ She used broken record when her mother came back with 'But you can't do THAT …' – page 100

▶ She encouraged herself beforehand. Sarah says, 'I was very nervous the day I decided to talk to her, and I kept consciously saying to myself, "I can do this. She's only a difficult old lady. All I've got to do is get a couple of sentences out and stick to my guns. I know I can do it, I've practised in class."' – page 72

▶ She focused on her body. 'All day I had to keep remembering to breathe. And when I arrived I sat in the car for a couple of minutes and breathed slowly and deeply. When I brought up the subject I was standing up and made sure I was standing straight. Just feeling my feet on the floor helped. I don't know how or why, but it did.' – page 66

▶ She thought through consequences. 'The worst that can happen is she behaves really badly, shouts and screams. She might say she never wants to see me again, but that's unlikely as I'm the only one who visits much anyway. And if she creates a great stink then I just refuse to go at all. I've got the trump card.' – page 103

▶ She set up support for herself. 'My assertiveness class were gunning for me to do it. I asked one of the women if I could call her on the day – before and after – to help talk me through it.' – page 142

▶ She stuck to her guns. 'Of course my mother played up a bit afterwards, telling me to go round immediately when it wasn't Tuesday, or asking me to do her shopping on other days of the week. I said, "I'll see you Tuesday" or "Tell me what you want and I'll bring it Tuesday." It was hard. I could feel myself wanting to cave in when she pushed the old buttons – saying she was ill or lonely – but I stuck with it and now our relationship is better than it has ever been. I'm sure she respects me more.' – page 99

▶ She took a risk. She tried something different. – page 105

▶ IT IMPROVED HER CONFIDENCE. – Every page!

Before, Sarah's mother was in charge and Sarah was running around after her. The 'relationship' was all about her mother and

there was no room for Sarah's wants, needs, preferences, opinions. By taking a stand, Sarah was *defining* herself. In effect she was
saying 'This is what I'm not willing to do/This *is* what I am willing
to do.' Psychotherapists call this 'setting boundaries' and psychotherapists are big on boundaries, because they work.
Whenever we set boundaries we are defining ourselves to the
world, stating what we will and will not do; what we want, and
what we don't want.

Penny was someone else who had to create some boundaries,
this time at work when she was promoted to office manager.
Before, she'd been 'one of the team'; now she was in charge. This
is always a tricky thing to negotiate. In my training, people bring
this problem up all the time: How do you handle managing your
'mates'?

One of Penny's 'mates', whom she was now in charge of, came to
her with a problem about another member of the management
team, one of Penny's new peers. Penny made the mistake of
sympathizing. Next thing she knew, her boss was saying 'What's
this I hear about you badmouthing other managers?'

After that, Penny had to set a boundary – that she wouldn't
gossip about other members of the management team to her
former 'mates'. This meant changing her behaviour: her old habits,
her inclination, was to gossip and sympathize. But she had to
maintain and respect her boundary – because her boundary
would protect her and keep her safe from more trouble.

Setting boundaries requires confidence. It requires that we
stretch our usual behaviour. But the payoffs are fantastic. And
boundaries do make us feel protected and secure.

Your Nine Relationship Rights

When I met Marcus I was, deep down, insecure and unsure of myself. The thing that attracted me to him was he was so intelligent, he knew so much about so many things. I was amazed he was interested in me, not that I showed it. At first the relationship seemed a razzle-dazzle of new things to know and learn about – his opinions on films were so interesting, our holidays were so exciting. I'd never met anyone like him and my life was transformed. Yet there were a few arguments at first – he had strong opinions on everything, including me. How I cooked, how I dressed, how I drove. It annoyed me, but I loved him so I didn't think it was a problem. Then, as a few years went by, and I took on a job that was a big challenge and rising to it made me feel more confident, I began to realize Marcus didn't like me having any opinion except his opinion, or doing anything anyway but his way. Our life was lived the way HE wanted it, not the way WE wanted it. And I began to question things, began to express differing opinions. We started to have terrible arguments and I got angrier and angrier as I realized no way was OK except his way and he wouldn't listen to what I wanted. Just as I was wondering what to do, he announced he'd been having an affair with his secretary and was leaving. I imagine he'd met someone who thought he was a god, like I used to.

And OK, I may have lost him, but my life is a million times better without him. Now I have a partner who respects my thoughts and opinions and I can dress, cook and drive however I like!

Jane, 36, reformed unconfident partner

As we've seen already, people who don't feel confident doubt themselves. They use up the energy output of your average power station wondering: 'Am I right to think this/want this/do this/say this?' And relationships offer a rich seam for doubting yourself.

So here, to help, are your rights as a partner in a confident relationship. They relate to relationships with lovers, family and friends; they will help you get clear about what you want and deserve, and believing in them will increase your confidence that you can deal with those unpredictable beasts – other people.

1   **The right to independence**

With parents this might mean the right to live your own life. In a love relationship it might mean the right to go out occasionally without him, the right to see your girlfriends, the right to time alone. Any relationship in which one member is prevented from truly being themselves and spending time separately from the relationship is not an equal relationship. It's a prison. Bullies and controlling people try to erode this right. When they do, they find out the controlled person grows to hate them for it.

2   **The right to be heard**

This involves the right to speak your truth – and be listened to. Not shouted down, dismissed, ignored or told to shut up. Plus the right to express your feelings and not be shouted down, told you or your feelings are stupid, talked over, etc.

3   **The right to create conflict**

Including the right to complain, disagree, rock the
boat. Remember Rosa and her mother's injunction:
'Don't start.' This is the right to start – and keep on
going – if that's what you need and what matters to
you.

4   **The right to say no**

Especially to sex when you don't feel like it, but also to
unreasonable parental demands. The right to not have
to spend Christmas with your family or even to see
your family if they're not respecting other rights.

5   **The right to have needs**

And maybe even collapse into a needy blob
occasionally. This includes being able to ask to get your
needs met. Needs for love, partnership, security –
whatever you need!

6   **The right to be treated with respect**

Again, this can have all kinds of corollaries, including
the right to security and fidelity within a love relationship – i.e. you are not being treated with respect if
your partner is constantly flirting with others or not
turning up when he says he will or, indeed, having sex
with someone else. Also abuse of any kind is certainly
not respect.

7　**The right to change yourself and try and improve the relationship**

Nuff said.

8　**The right to equality**

The right for all parties in a relationship to matter equally – in terms of time, attention, needs. It is not an equal relationship if one partner feels – and acts – superior and another partner feels – and acts – inferior.

9　**The right to end the relationship if it's not working for you**

Remember that teenager who divorced his parents in America? This one can apply to family relationships and friendships as well as love gone bad. And you have the right to end a relationship without being stalked, coerced, threatened or any nasties like that. If things are really bad; if your father hits you, your partner or any family member abuses you in any way – insults you, hurts you, steals money from you – you have the right to end the relationship.

Also remember the other detailed, specific rights in Chapter 3 which have a bearing on our relationships. Like the right to make a mistake or to change your mind.

☆ Star Tip

Any violation of these nine relationship rights requires a confident response from you.

Something to Think About

Sometimes unconfident people secretly want to be looked after. They attract their opposites – people who appear strong and appear to have it all sorted. Then, when the honeymoon's over, cracks often appear. The one who wanted to be looked after may become resentful if their expectations of being cared for aren't met. Or the other person gets fed up with having to be the strong, rescuing party. Or they boss and control the one who wanted to be looked after so much they fall out of love with them. Then, once again, that person ends up 'disappointed'.

Equally often, unconfident people find someone *they* can look after, then later find they're fed up with doing all the giving and getting nothing back.

If either of these sounds familiar, look at who you are choosing. What do you really want and what do you secretly want? Is there a conflict?

Exercise

Ponder these questions:

Who in my life is violating any of my relationship rights?

_____

What are the payoffs for me putting up with this?
Negative   Positive

_____

What do I want to do about it? (e.g. say something to them? See less of them? End the relationship? Suggest couples counselling?)

_____

What am I going to do in the next week/month to tackle this issue?

_____

How will I support myself in tackling this? Help includes using breathing and clear communication, discussing it first with a supportive friend, phoning a friend before and after, etc.

_____

When am I going to tackle this? (e.g. by the end of next week, next month)

_____

How committed (marks out of 10, with 10 representing very committed) am I to tackling this?

_____

What treat will I give myself afterwards?

_____

15

Dealing with Difficult Friends

A good friendship is when we can both be true to ourselves.
Whether that's via our belief system, our thoughts or feelings,
our behaviour or in our sense of what it is we want to do. No
matter on what level, if we're really true to ourselves then the
friendship will build. It can accommodate change. Sometimes
then I will do something for you because I believe in it and
sometimes you'll do the same for me. If I help you out when
you're ill it's because I feel comfortable and clear that that's what
I've chosen to do. Even if it's tough for me and I might moan
about it!

**Maggie McKenzie, Director at the Spectrum Psychotherapy
Centre in London**

I was in the final throes of splitting up from my soon-to-be ex-
husband. I'd had a dreadful night – he woke me up shouting that,
for the past couple of weeks, I had behaved 'like a robot'. So I did
what a girl does when she's desperate. I rang my best friend. But.
My friend's response was: 'Poor him. If you were behaving like that,
I'd want to slap you round the face.'

To which my response went something like 'Whaaat!!?!!! It's not
your job to say "Poor him." It's your job as my best friend to say,
"Poor you." And then, I think, I slammed the phone down.

At that time, I had known her for 12 years and had been speak-
every-day close for five. We'd been typical best friends, supporting one another through ups and downs, boys and joys, holidays

and hangovers. I have always secretly envied her ability to call a spade not just a spade but a blunt instrument with poo on it. We've shared endless laughs when sometimes her 'blurts' come out just plain tactless. But I didn't like it when her talent was focused on me at a time when I was feeling very vulnerable.

It was the first time we'd had real differences. I felt like my world was shifting under me. Not only was I ending a marriage that had only lasted a year; now I was falling out with my best friend. At least I was not alone. Maggie McKenzie, the psychotherapist quoted at the start of this chapter, says it's classically when other changes happen (like one person becoming more confident) that friendships hit sticky patches. 'Usually what happens with friend-ships is you meet and whatever it is you're doing – work, college, for example – connects you up; it's like the beginning of any other relationship. Dynamics of difficulty arrive when something changes. One person makes changes in their love relationship, or they have a relationship when they've been single, or they move house or job, or they go into therapy, or someone dies. Then you really see who your friend is. The old saying that you know who your friends are in a crisis is really true.'

Our crisis was three years ago now – and, yes, we are still good friends. Along with making the decision to end my marriage, repairing and remaining with my best-friendship has been one of the most difficult relationship challenges I've ever tackled.

It's taken a hell of a lot of cups of tea and talking. Hours spent exploring what was going on between us. It has taken patience, forgiveness, forbearance, love – all those qualities, in fact, you're supposed to muster for marriage.

It has felt very grown-up to allow differences into the relationship and admit that, no, we might not like everything the other does, but we love each other anyway.

Getting to grips with difficult days is to friendship what years in a cellar is to fine wine. Maggie McKenzie says, 'Often as young people we base relationships on "Be like me" or "I want to be like you." We do that because our identity is unstable and we're still forming it. But if a relationship stays based on "Be like me" it's not going to develop. When one friend gets a better job or starts or ends a relationship and the other disapproves, there may not be the support and affection any more.

'But if we can develop ourselves and our friendships to a place where you can say "This is who I am, I see who you are and our differences," then how we between us handle a challenging life-situation will be interesting and informative and deepen the friendship. The wise message is develop those "This is who I am and I see who you are" conversations and the friendship will endure.'

Your difficulties with friends can be that they *always* fall into one of these five types below. Or they can be this way *sometimes*. When the friendship scales tip out of balance, here's how to cope:

The Too-honest Friend

OK, so my best friend is one of these. They have their plus points – you always know where you are with them; you never get to go out looking like the back end of a hippopotamus. But when you're in the doldrums, they are like chillis, to be used sparingly. What motivates them? Honesty. As my best friend says: 'If I can't say what I think and mean with you, then what's the point?'

Life coach Bob Griffiths agrees: 'I was with a group of people once and a man said, "I really want to be attractive to women," and one of the women said, "I have to tell you if you want to be attractive to women you have to stop dressing like a complete slob." It was the truth told absolutely brutally. And there can be great value in this. Someone who cuts to the core of something can be fantastically valuable and powerful.'

Making It Work

▶ Bob's tip for dealing with the too-honest friend is this: 'You have to be allowed to express your own feelings. Most very truthful people are very confident and have great self-esteem and not a great sense of what goes on for other people. You have to tell them when they've gone over the top and hurt you. On the other hand, I hedge slightly, some people are brutal and stupid, and some are brutal and very incisive. You have to be able to tell the difference.'

▶ Take a leaf out of the honest friend's book and tell her when she goes too far. When I do this with my best friend she always squeals: 'Ooh, I should have done it nicer. It'll be on my gravestone: *she should have done it nicer.*'

The Do-as-I-Say Friend

This friend uses words like 'should' and 'ought' and makes liberal use of the phrase 'If I were you …' – which is fine if you've asked. But maybe you haven't. Do-as-I-say friends often have wisdom in abundance, but not enough to notice when they spiral out of control. Which they are especially prone to when you're in a mess and they are not. As Amanda, 26, says, 'I have a friend at work like this. We've worked together for ages, but now that she's leaving, every time we have a chat she tells me I ought to get out too, and she tells me whom I should talk to, and how I should go about it. But I don't *want* to leave.'

Bossy friends don't listen, they dictate. Often all we need is to pour out our woes, without someone else coaching us like she's a football manager and it's two minutes to the cup final.

Making It Work

▶ Boss her back and tell her to butt out. Bossiness, says psychotherapist and coach Sandra Donaldson, is 'a real test of whether we stay true to ourselves or whether we give in and keep the peace'. She says: 'In all these friend- ship issues the answer is about putting the issue on the table and talking about it. And not having expectations of the other to change. Many relationships break down because two people have different expectations of one another or different styles of going about things. It's a real test of friendship when you don't expect change and you're willing to live with the differences.'

▶ Don't be afraid of the consequences. Sandra says: 'Relationships with friends are like those with lovers – they get to a stage where need to deepen, and often they deepen through conflict. For me, the lesson has been that we can be in conflict and still build this great friendship. It builds more trust in. Anger can be a great energy in a relationship, but can also be a wedge if not used productively. Productively means I need to tell you I'm angry with you, otherwise I'll snipe or talk about you behind your back. And that doesn't do you or me any good.'

▶ Often bossiness is a bossy friend's way of showing she cares. So tell her what *would* help. Bob Griffiths says conflict is increased by focusing on what you *don't* want. Tell her *how* she could help. Like, 'I'd like you to just listen while I explore this for myself.'

▶ Is she merely bossy, or a bully? Bullies tend to insult, belittle and generally make you feel like a termite if you don't do what they say. Bossy friends just boss you, but still have goodwill. Bullies don't. Use your gut instincts to tell you which she is.

▶ Turn it into a joke, as in (said in a jokey, affectionate tone of voice) 'There you go telling me what to do again ...'

The Me-Me-Me Friend

She never stops talking, and the talk is all about her. She is liable to call and ask you to drop everything to come shopping/ go dancing/get dressed up, there's a love, and get round here immediately because her latest crush is in the bar round the corner and she needs back-up. The upside of the demanding friend is she's often the life and soul of the party. The downside: you really have to be able to hold your own or you'll find your-self growing tufts and sitting inside the front door waiting for her to wipe her feet on you.

Mary, 31, says: 'I adore my sister-in-law, but she gets a bit much if you don't know how to deal with her. One time she got me to pick her up from Heathrow and we were driving through London and got stuck in traffic. Sitting in the back seat she said "Is this the best way to get through London?" and because I was stressed, I exploded. "Perhaps you should have got a taxi and they would have found a better way. As it is I'm driving and giving up my day to help you out, so you go the way I decide on." She hasn't asked me to do anything for her since then.'

Making It Work

▶ Ask yourself how demanding is *too* demanding. Bob Griffiths says, 'If I had a client complaining to me about their demanding friend, I'd be quite brutal with them. I'd ask, what's it like being treated as a doormat? What do you get out of it? I'd be helping them establish boundaries. Everybody needs some kind of standard. It's good to be aware of how you want and need be treated. The higher standards you have, the better people treat you. There's an unconscious knowing that goes on when you allow people to treat you badly. People will consciously or unconsciously take advantage of you if they can.'

▶ Notice if it's a rigid pattern. Does the demanding all go one way? Or do you get to have her at your command occasionally?

▶ If it is a recurring one-sided pattern you need to learn to say no. Bob Griffiths says, 'This is about starting to stand up for yourself and learning that the world does not fall apart when you say no.' Have a look at page 102 and remind yourself about saying no.

▶ When she's rattling on, interrupt with 'Enough about you already. Now I want to tell you about *my* day.'

▶ Maggie McKenzie says, 'Is a demanding friend someone who asks a lot for themselves or asks a lot of you? It may be that you need it. If someone is fairly passive in their life, and their friend who goes out a lot says "I've two tickets for movies, or on Sunday there's a play and I've organized for us to go, it'll be fun," is that friend too demanding? The person who's being passive and likes to lie around may end up saying "you're too demanding for me." So if you look at someone and think they're too demanding you may also have to admit you're not active enough.'

The My-Life's-a-Plight Friend

Usually, when we make friends with someone, it's because we're both in the same boat, whatever kind of choppy waters we might be negotiating. It can be very tricky when one finds a lifeline and the other's still thrashing around. As Lucy, 30, found out when she 'settled down'. She says, 'I find one of my friends socially embarrassing now. I didn't notice when I was single, it was a laugh. But now she seems to be off her face all the time and I find myself saying things like, "I can't believe you got so drunk you fell over and showed him your knickers." Part of me feels so loyal, she really was there for me when I was single. But now I've moved on it's such a wedge between us.'

One of the trickiest aspects of the my-life's-a-plight friend is when they get into difficulties you personally disapprove of. Jane, 27, says, 'One of my friends is having an on-off affair with a married man. I'm friends with her boyfriend too, and I do find it very difficult. I've tried to be level with her and not judgemental, and also not bust her secret. She's needed a lot of support, but sometimes I feel like saying, "What the f*** are you doing, you stupid cow? You're ruining your life! Grow up." But I have learned to listen and keep schtum.'

Of course we all go through my-life's-a-plight periods, but some pals can get stuck in the mire so that each time you meet up, there's some new murky tale.

Making It Work

▶ You don't want to turn into a do-as-I-say friend, but maybe your moaning minnie needs a bit of tough love. If you're not sure what I mean, read the too-honest friend section above and ask are you being honest enough?

▶ Ask *yourself* some tough questions: Does having them in your life make you feel better? Are you rescuing them? Would your anxiety lessen if you could just accept that this is how they are and you cannot change them? If you couldn't sort them out, would you still be interested? Be careful that you're not in the role of rescuer or, indeed, do-as-I-say friend. Bob Griffiths says, 'Some people get something out of complaining, they like to see themselves as downtrodden, a victim. Then the pattern of downtrodden victim behaviour becomes part of their identity. Other people get their self-esteem from helping other people, but before you know it you're sucked in constantly doing stuff, constantly supporting them and you feel resentful in the end.'

The Stirrer

The stirrer is never happy unless there's a huge drama going on. If there isn't, she'll create one.

Susan, 35, says, 'When my difficult friend's life is in a mess, she tries to interfere with mine. So she'll pick over my situation until she finds something. I may have made a passing comment; she'll dig it around, pull it about and make a big issue about it, then come out with huge words of wisdom. For example, I recently met a man

and she knows his ex-wife. So she says, "His ex can be very difficult, if she found out he's going out with someone as fabulous as
you she might really play up."

'I stopped her in her tracks. I said, first, his ex is none of my business; second, if there are problems with her it's for him to sort
out. She comes back with "Oh, I just don't want you to get hurt."
Actually she's stirring. But she is good and a nice friend most of
the time.'

Making It Work

▶   When you come across a stirrer, or a friend who is
     stirring, the adage is, just say no. Don't get hooked.
     Susan says, 'When my friend starts stirring, it often
     ends with me saying "This is none of your business"
     and that's very difficult. She finds it very difficult too.
     But it's the only way.'

▶   Ask them what's going on. Get them to question
     themselves about why they are looking for trouble in
     your life. You could get some interesting answers.

▶   Again, make a joke, but make a point. You could say,
     'Ooh, you're just trying to stir up a drama. Get
     yourself on *EastEnders*.'

❧ So What Is a Good Friend?
Which Friendships Are Worth Sticking with?

You might have difficulties with your too honest, overly bossy,
life's-a-plight friend, but what makes her worth the distance?
Both Maggie McKenzie and Sandra Donaldson cite 'goodwill'.
That is, the ability to maintain a positive attitude towards one

another no matter what else might be going on between you. It's about feeling and believing your friend is basically a good person, and has your interests at heart, even if right now they're going through a demanding phase, or their life is such a mess they have no energy left over for yours. The key is that we can be ourselves, however we are, and it's OK.

☆ **Star Tip**

You need to steer clear of anyone who erodes your confidence in any way and in any area, no matter how long you've known them. Back away.

Exercise

Ponder these questions:

Who in my life fits any of these categories?

_____

What are the payoffs for me putting up with this?

Negative   Positive

_____

What do I want to do about that?:

▶   Say something to them?
▶   See less of them?

What am I going to do in the next week/month to tackle this issue?

_____

How will I support myself in tackling this? (Breathing and clear communication, discussing it first with another supportive friend, phoning another friend before and after, etc.)

_____

When am I going to tackle this? (e.g. by the end of next week, next month)

_____

How committed (marks out of 10, with 10 representing very committed) am I to tackling this?

_____

What treat will I give myself afterwards?

_____

16

In the Family Firing Line

How to stay confident in the face of ancient
family patterns

> If there was one person who could knock all the confidence out
> of me no matter what, it was my Dad. He left when I was 10
> and I didn't see him too often after that, and whenever I did I was
> desperate for him to take notice of me. I think I blamed myself
> for him going, but I kind of idolized him and I'd try really hard
> to impress him. But he'd always cut me down with just one
> remark. I realize now he is and has always been a critical bug-
> ger, and he knows how to go for the jugular. He has an instinct
> for it. Over the years I've realized that what he says isn't neces-
> sarily true, it's him being bitter and critical. So now when he crit-
> icizes me I don't take it personally any more, and I come back
> with remarks like, 'That was a horrible thing to say' or 'Oh, so
> you think that, do you?' or even 'I'm not interested in hearing
> you criticize me.' It does knock the wind out of his sails.
>
> Knowing I can come back has changed the whole way I see him. I
> see him as a bitter old man and I can even laugh at the outrageous
> things he says.
>
> Lucy, 32, on changing your reactions to relatives

A lot of what we've said about friendships is relevant to family
relationships and to romantic partnerships. You might have a Me-
Me-Me mother, or a sister who's a stirrer, a sister-*in-law* who's a
stirrer or a partner who bosses you about. Also, family members

may regularly ignore your relationship rights – a mother who won't let you be yourself, or won't accept who you really are, or a father who won't let you disagree with him and won't listen to you if you try and express your anger about that.

When we don't feel confident in relationships it's because we doubt ourselves, we're not sure if our decisions, approach, desires, wants and needs are the right ones. And it may be we don't feel we know how to do relationships. Plus if our self-esteem is wobbly we may complicate all this still further by blaming ourselves, putting ourselves in the wrong.

Building a confident self in relationships involves constant practice of many of the techniques mentioned in this book so far: clear, direct communication, believing you matter and you are important, setting boundaries, being clear about how far you will go, and up with what you will not put!

Our families can be the hottest, most challenging place of all to act with more confidence. That's because our families are usually where we learned any unconfident patterns of behaviour/thinking/beliefs in the first place, and patterns of behaviour become deeply ingrained over the years. But if we can change patterns here, we can change patterns anywhere. The many people I know who have tackled their family difficulties with more confidence have experienced enormous benefits. Like Lucy, whose quote began this chapter, and who adds: 'The first time I ever stood up to my father I thought the world might end. But it didn't and now he knows I won't take any shit from him any longer he seems to respect me more and treats me more like an equal. As a result, I don't hate or fear or idolize him any more and we've become closer. So the fear and difficulty I felt when I first started answering him back was well worth it.'

Q. My dad has been bossing me all my life. How can I change something like that which is so old and deep?

The answer: drawing a line under what has gone before.

You can change your behaviour any place, any time.

Unhealthy/negative relationship patterns become ingrained. But either side can do something different at any time which breaks the pattern. If you've always, say, slipped into Rebellious child (see page 88), then the next time your father starts bossing, you come back with an adult response. For example: listening to him, if what you usually do is interrupt and storm out, and then saying something like 'Well, you've a right to your opinion' and staying (appearing to stay!) calm. This will knock him off his feet because this is not how he's used to you reacting, and he'll have to have a different response himself. He may rant and say 'Yes, that is my opinion, blah blah blah' but if you again sit tight and have a different reaction to the one you usually have, you've already changed the relationship in that moment.

The Key: Do Something Different

Where does your difficulty come from? Think back to the material on transactional analysis on page 85 and identify which mode you're in. Or are you playing victim (page 23). Then do something different.

> ▶ If you're moaning, letting other people sort you out and tell you what to do …
> Take some action and do something for yourself; tell others 'I can cope on my own, thank you.'

▶ If you're criticizing, telling others what to do, blaming ...
STOP – and form some adult response. Listen and/or support them instead.

▶ If you're feeling like a dogsbody, bailing others out financially or otherwise ...
STOP and practise saying no (page 102)

What You Can Do

▶ Define your core message and either deliver it at an appropriate moment or when an appropriate moment is sprung upon you.

▶ Be prepared. Know that a difficult family member can be difficult at any time. So think through possible difficulties and comebacks beforehand so you know how you might react with confidence. This avoids that, 'Oh, why did I say *that*'? syndrome.

▶ Make sure your behaviour and what you say are congruent. Otherwise you'll be giving out mixed messages.

▶ Stick to your guns. It's often not the first time you do something different that's truly hard, but the second, third and fourth times.

▶ Try, as much as you can, not to get into hot conversations with *other* family members. For example, moaning to your sister about your mum, or siding with your mum against your sister. Make like Switzerland and stay neutral. Siding with one person against another is called 'triangling' and only ever results in more misery.

▶ Do ask for support, though, from other family members or friends *whom you can rely on to be supportive*. If your sister is understanding, by all means

let her know you're trying to break the pattern of
someone else bullying you and you're trying to stand
up for yourself. Don't, however, do this unless you can
truly trust them.

Warning! The Change-back reaction

When we change family or relationship patterns, we are challenging modes of behaviour which go very deep indeed. And
because they go very deep, the level of anxiety when they are
challenged is high. Not just for you but for other people too. So
expect them to have a big reaction. They may:

▶   get ill
▶   get worse – behave more badly
▶   cut you off
▶   create more conflict

for a while. Your challenge is to stick to your guns and not get
fazed by the change into going back to how things were before.
That's *why* they're behaving like this.

I first learned about the 'change-back' reaction in psychologist
Harriett Goldhor Lerner's book, *The Dance of Intimacy*. She
writes, 'It is important to keep in mind that countermoves or
"Change back!" reactions occur whenever we moves toward a
higher level of assertiveness, separateness and maturity in a key
relationship. When we are the one initiating a change, we easily
forget that countermoves express anxiety, not lack of love, and
they are always predictable.'

Your job is to hold tight. Remember:

▶ The world will not end if you decide not to go to that second cousin's wedding (or whatever it is).

▶ People respect other people who stand their ground and stand up for themselves. *Even when those people don't like it.*

However, what makes the 'change back' reaction tricky is that it might also occur in you. It may take the form of doubts, criticism, your inner critic having a field day. The minute you do that thing you've been using all your confidence techniques to build up to, instead of praising yourself, you start thinking: 'Oh, maybe I was wrong, I shouldn't have done that …' and a million mad thoughts go through your head. Or it might take the form of a dull ache in the pit of your stomach. Or *you* might get ill.

☆ Star Tip

This is only resistance. It might feel real, but it is only resistance. Stick to your guns, remember all the reasons you wanted to change things, get out your list of payoffs and stare at it. Tell a friend you're having this reaction and get reassurance you've done the right thing. Whatever you do, don't go back on yourself.

Exercise

Ponder these questions:

What are my unconfident habits/behaviours with friends? _____
_____
… with lovers/partners? _____
… with family? _____

What are the payoffs for me putting up with the three worst relationship issues I have right now?

Negative _____ Positive _____

What 10 small changes in relationships would I like to make?

_____

What 10 big changes in relationships would I like to make?

_____

What do I want to do about it? (e.g. Say something to them? try something different) _____

_____

What am I going to do in the next week/month to tackle this issue? _____

_____

How will I support myself in tackling this? (Breathing and clear communication, discussing it first with a supportive friend, phoning a friend before and after, etc.) _____

_____

What encouraging statements can I make to support myself in doing this? _____

_____

When am I going to tackle this? (e.g. by the end of next week, next month) _____

_____

How committed (marks out of 10, with 10 representing very committed) am I to tackling this? _____

What treat will I give myself afterwards? _____

17

The Shy Girl's Guide to Finding Love

Women don't lose out by making the first move. Yes, it's scary, but you can't sit around passively and wait to be noticed.
Sharyn Wolf, author of *Guerrilla Dating Tactics*

... and who isn't shy when it comes to looking for love?

You like him. You like the way he looks, he smiles. You've spoken and nothing went horribly wrong. You'd like to take it further. Now what? Do you wait for him to make the first move? Which could be never. Or do you do something about it?

Asking a man out requires all the confidence techniques you can muster. I know. I've done it. Up until January 1996 I'd never asked a man out, I'd only gone out with men who picked me. This was something my therapist pointed out when I was having a moan about the parlous state of my love life. She said, 'The guy says "I want you" and you say "OK." You don't ask yourself, "Is this a good person for me?" It's very passive.' Hmmm. Never one to let something lie once it has been drawn to my attention, I decided to try something different. I decided to ask out a man who didn't even know me.

I'd gone to a wedding and spotted a cute guy with a smile to melt a copper kettle. Weeks later, drooling over the wedding pictures with my friend who'd got married, I said, 'Who's that? I like *him*.'

My friend, as married friends will, said, 'That's Jonathan's friend and he's single.'

To cut a long story short, they offered to fix me up on a blind date. Her husband, Jonathan, rang the cute guy and told him I was interested. Cute guy didn't remember me from the wedding (great) but was interested (great!). 'Give me her number, I'll call her' said Mr X. Jonathan said he'd check with me.

He did check with me and the prospect filled me with ohmigod anxiety. What if he rang when I was out? Or naked? Or giggling with my best friend? Or all three? It seemed odd, having made the first move myself, to then expect him to call. It seemed, well, passive.

So I decided to call *him*. I let a week go by, then I chose six o'clock on a Saturday evening, usually a good time for finding people in. I read my horoscope: 'A good day for taking the initiative,' it said. 'Create the right environment and anything is possible.'

So I put on Massive Attack, lit a candle, primed my best friend so I could call her for support afterwards, did some deep breathing for a few minutes (not too long, or you persuade yourself not to do it), felt my feet on the floor and dialled that number.

It felt a bit like an out-of-body experience, hearing the phone ring and then hearing his voice, I was so spacey with anxiety. But I was feeling the fear and doing it anyway.

'Hi, is that Matthew? I'm Jonathan's friend, the one he told you about.'

Big silence. *Huge* silence.

'Er, he *did* tell you about me, didn't he? I'm the one …'

'Yes! I was going to call him and get your number.'

'Well, I was the one who made the initial impetus (hey, I was *nervous*) for this thing, so I thought it was only fair that I ring you.'

'Brilliant! But women don't do this!'

'This woman's never done it before.'

'Men love it!' (Meaning *he* loved it.)

'Great. That makes me slightly less nervous.' (Meaning 99 per cent nervous as opposed to 100 per cent. My heart was pounding like a Megadeth bassline.)

We arranged to meet that week. And my taking the initiative resulted in a relationship that lasted two and a half years.

But what if he'd said no? Or we'd had a disastrous first date? Well, as someone pointed out to me once, no one ever died of rejection. No one ever died of a disastrous first date, either. I did decide that if it went badly, I had nothing to lose and I wouldn't take it personally. And that *is* a decision. Yes, it would have been embarrassing, but I thought through the consequences of not doing it and also decided, as Susan Jeffers advises, 'Whatever happens, I'll handle it.'

The Shy Girl's Tips for Making Man-contact

▶ Obviously, find out if he's available. You'll save yourself the pain of rejection due to sheer inappropriateness.

▶ Smile. Make eye contact. The possibility of romance makes even ballsy girls quake and display classic shyness symptoms. But flirting begins with these two basics.

▶ Just do it. Let him know you like him somehow. Ask him to a movie, or to some group activity coming up.

▶ If you can't stand the thought of coming out with it to his face, get his email address and ask that way, or leave a message on his answerphone at a time you know he'll be out. If neither of these is possible, you could resort to the old 'my friend likes you' tactic and get a friend to ask him, bearing in mind it's horribly teenage and a thousand teen movies have revolved around the things that can go wrong.

▶ When you are talking to him, use the tactics in this book. Breathe, feel your feet on the floor, stand up straight, keep communication clear and don't gabble.

▶ Do express your nervousness. Let him see it's a big deal for you to be saying this: 99 per cent of men will be flattered.

▶ Don't worry about what is a good opening line, just say what feels right to you.

▶ When you ask, be specific. 'Would you like to see a film this Friday?' is more likely to get results than 'Would you like to see a film some time?'

▶ Set up some support for before and afterwards with a confidence buddy.

▶ If he does say no or fobs you off, the confident response would be something like 'Oh well, never mind' delivered lightly. Then get out of there – fast (but confidently!).

▶ Do not obsess afterwards about how you could have done it better and how you *should* have said blah blah. Just praise yourself for having done it at all.

▶ Ditto don't obsess about *him*. It's best to try and leave nothing loose or open to interpretation, but if he says, 'I'll call you,' then doesn't, *that means he's not interested*. It is unlikely to mean he's lost your number, or got held up at work all week or has been in a nasty accident or whatever.

Be brave.

Body Language That Tells You He's Interested

▶ Eye contact. He fixes you with a steely gaze and keeps it going for far longer than would, say, the postman.

▶ He strokes his neck. New research on flirting says that, in the presence of a woman a man finds attractive, he indulges in instinctive, universal mating behaviour that puts him on a level with a male peacock. He arches his back, stretches his pecs, imperceptibly sways his pelvis in a tame Elvis impression, swaggers and laughs extra loudly.

▶ He makes grand gestures. He whips out his cigarette lighter with a flourish and flicks it on like he's auditioning for one of those old silent movies. He tugs his tie and chugs his chin toward the ceiling. What's happening is that an ancient part of his brain is enacting an urban pantomime of the kind of stuff randy apes get up to in the jungle.

▶ His pupils enlarge. Apparently this happens so the eye can take in more of the beloved object. Bear in mind, though, it's hard to tell in a nightclub. It may be a sign he's taken too many Es and is off his head.

▶ He touches or strokes his glass, his hand, his neck. One giveaway of body language is our miniature gestures echo the larger gestures we'd like to make if we weren't so inhibited. Ergo he strokes his glass because he'd like to be stroking you.

▶ He touches you in conversation. As above, only he's getting a little braver.

▶ He mirrors your body language. You move forward, he moves forward; you cross your legs, he crosses his.

Now for the opposite problem: when he's oh-so-interested, and you're not.

Saying No Gracefully

I have friends who will go out with anyone because they can't turn anyone down, they are too flattered to say no. It doesn't say anything about you when some spotty, paunchy twit fancies you. There are ways of being approached by a man that are actually insulting.
Sarah, 23, hardline naysayer

So, a really nice guy gives you the chat. He's pleasant, he's keen, but he's wearing Hush Puppies. Or his halitosis would frighten your cats. Or you're not sure what it is but whatever it is he just isn't *you*.

He asks for your number. Are you gonna be nice? Or are you gonna be honest?

Just recall what happens when you say yes but you mean no. Every time the phone rings your stomach gets a little sinking feeling. It might be your mother. It might be your best friend. But, it might also be *him*. So you don't answer the phone and suddenly you're a prisoner in your own home. Or you do answer the phone and it's him and you find yourself saying, 'Yes, all right' and then, *oh my God!* Or 'Yes, all right, but not this week' and somehow he never gets the message and you have visions of yourself at 70 with a zimmer frame picking up the handpiece and saying, 'Sorry not this week …'

Plus, maybe you have to avoid all your favourite haunts in case he's there.

Do you really want your social life to be this complicated?

There are ways of letting him down gently so he doesn't feel like Quasimodo and you don't feel a heel. All men agree they'd rather get a quick no than a fruitless runaround. But who wants to hear the blunt, God's honest truth – I don't find you attractive? You don't want to say it, he certainly doesn't want to hear it.

Tried and Tested Lines

The #1 Favourite Little White Lie

▶ Sorry, I've got a boyfriend/I live with someone/I'm married. He wouldn't like it if I gave you my number/went out with you.

If He Knows You're Single …

▶ Sorry, I've just split up with someone and I know I'm not ready to see anyone.
▶ You're lovely, but you're just not my type.
▶ You're lovely, but you're just like my brother and it would be like incest(!)
▶ Sorry, I'm just too busy at the moment.

► I'm sorry, I just don't give out my phone number.
(Some women do make it a personal policy not to
give out their number – it's kind of obvious, though,
that if you fancied the pants off him you'd be
scribbling on the nearest matchbox.)

If He Persists

► Try saying, 'Why don't I take *your* number?' You're
saying you'll take it. You're not saying you'll *use* it.

► Body language. Try and look relaxed. Smile and make
eye contact. Keep your voice calm and say something
like, 'Thanks. I'm flattered. But I'm very busy.' Don't
speak too quickly, and respond with a downward
inflection on the word 'busy' while maintaining eye
contact. This shows authority and shows you mean
business. (Or, rather, not.)

► Keep it light. Smile. If you're a joker, make a joke.
Humour always takes the tension out.

Don't:

► Overexplain. Recall the maxim: never apologize, never
explain. Apologize if you want, but don't get caught up
in 'My boss is making me work all hours and although
I'd love to I'm really exhausted and ... and ...' It only
prolongs the agony.

► Use the word 'can't' – it sounds passive and suggests
you'd like to but cannot. Which gives him an opening
to persuade you you can really or you could later.

Remember:

> You are not responsible for his feelings.
> You have the right to say no.
> You have the right to spend your time as you see fit.

And what if you did say yes and have been chewing the carpet ever since? You also have the right to change your mind. Everyone does, all the time. Call him back and say, 'Sorry, but I've been thinking about it and I was wrong to say yes, I really don't want to see you I'd really rather not meet up.' Or if you can't get his number, turn up on the date and say you've changed your mind and you're going back home. The world will not end.

Otherwise you get his hopes up for nothing. Wouldn't you rather be let down gently than be given the runaround?

Dating

> If a man comes on to you, even if you're glad of the attention, for God's sake try and hide that. You should behave as though that's your due, which it is. For *everyone*. We all have something about us which can enchant, but if you behave like it's a huge compliment that someone's noticed it, you really are short-changing yourself.
>
> **Maria, 23, hard line advocate of dating confidently**

Dating, believe it or not, is supposed to be fun. So don't take it all deadly seriously.

The world does not begin and end with this date. You're just meeting up with someone. You are not a contestant in the date Olympics, competing to be the prettiest, wittiest, most perfect date ever (oh, and potential mother of generations). Acting as though you are raises the stakes sky high.

You're just having a coffee with another human being who happens to be a man.

Just enjoy it.

Yes, dating can give you the most thrilling feelings of excitement and exhilaration when it goes right, and the most appalling downers when it goes badly. The trick is to minimize the downer dates and up your chances of hitting a bullseye. Fortunately you have the all tools to do this right now. You just may have to go down the shed and give some of them a good old polish.

The dating arena is an excellent place to practise your new skills: Your self-awareness. Your knowing what you want and need. Your courage in speaking up and stating it. And all the other techniques you've learned so far.

The advantage of becoming more clear and assertive is, once you feel the thrill it gives you, once you experience of how much easier it makes your life, you start using it all over the place. With your boss, with your mother, the man who comes to sell dusters at the door, whoever.

Work That Flirting Muscle!

We all know someone who attracts men like flies, even when she's no Michelle Pfeiffer. I know a woman who will turn up at a club in a track suit top and chinos when all the other women look like they've dressed for the Oscars, and within minutes she'll be surrounded by men. It's something in the way she holds herself. The way she looks entirely comfortable with herself, even when dressed all 'wrong'. She looks relaxed, happy, approachable. The message she gives out is: 'I like myself. I bet you'd like me too.'

It's called confidence.

Before Your Date

▶ Make sure you look the best you possibly can. Get yourself a makeover. Get yourself a new haircut. Go to a shop and get them to tell you the clothes that look best on you. Treat yourself to a visit with an image consultant like Color Me Beautiful (Call 0207 627 5211 for your nearest consultant). Looking the best you can is all part of loving yourself. You always feel more confident when you know you look good.

▶ Get your friends to tell you what your strong points are – and enhance them.

▶ Make some confidence-boosting affirmations. Look back on the work you did on beliefs in Chapter 7. Tell yourself you're confident, sexy, intelligent, funny, witty, smart.

▶ Wear red. It's a bright, sexy, confident colour. Notice how you feel in different colours.

▶ Wear red lipstick.

▶ Get fit. Get your body looking the best it can. Dress so you enhance your body's good points.

▶ Relax. Be gorgeous. Be yourself – if you're a bubbly personality, bubble. If you're normally quiet, shut up.

▶ **Have a laugh.** A straw poll of men questioned for my last book said the ability to make them laugh was far more important in a woman than breast size. Hmmm. Anyway. Learn some jokes. One of my friends

has a humour habit that sends men weak at the knees
every time.

► Remind yourself: **I'm not here to make this
work, but to see if I like this person or not. If
it doesn't feel good, I won't do it again.**

► Remember, he's doubtless nervous too!

☆ Star Tip

Whatever you do, wherever you go, do let someone else
(apart from him) know what you're doing and where you're
going. This is a safety mechanism all dating agencies advise.
Tell them when you're expected home. Just in case …

What to Say

Whether your first date is shopping at Tesco or tea at the Ritz
the only thing that matters is you both give good talk.

Do:

► Offer him a compliment. Often the first thing a man
says on a first date is 'like the dress'. If he doesn't, he
should. Yet how often do we return the compliment?
One of the men I interviewed for my last book said,
'I hate how we're expected to make all the effort. If a
woman compliments me it says three things. It tells
me she's confident, she's nice and not a frosty ice
maiden and, most importantly, she's keen, which puts
me at my ease.'

► Be yourself. If he mentions his first from Cambridge
don't start making out you're a great intellectual
yourself. If it sounds like he spends his whole life
following Arsenal don't feign an interest in sport you

don't feel. If he doesn't like you for who you are, he isn't right for you.

▶ Tell him you're nervous (if you are). As we know from Part One, speaking your feelings helps to make them go away. And if he admits to nerves too, you'll feel closer to one another. If he responds by trying to make you *more* nervous, well, you know then what to think of *him*.

▶ Ask him how he thinks and feels. The two questions: 'Oh, yes, and how do you feel about that?' and 'What do you think about that?' can reveal bucketloads about your potential mate. On a first date, I once asked a man how he felt about something that had happened to him and he answered, 'I don't know. I never know what I'm feeling.' He was right. And I was about to discover it's not easy having a relationship with someone who never knows if they're angry or ecstatic.

▶ Touch him. Touching establishes intimacy, demonstrates warmth and presumes familiarity. Which is a wonderful cure for first-night nerves.

▶ Listen!

Don't:

▶ Bombard him with questions that point to an above-average interest in whether he'll make a good life partner. Show an interest, but don't be too nosy or intrusive too soon. Some over-the-top women can frighten men to death.

▶ Talk, talk, talk. It's a feminine trait, especially when nervous, to yak as though you were practising for the European Yakking Championships. But how are you going to find out about *him*?

▶ Mention the M word, as in, 'Last Saturday I went to my sister's wedding.'

▶ Be frightened of silence.

▶ Rattle on about exes. Remember the *Friends* episode where Rachel on a first date chattered incessantly about how she was over Ross? It is not a good idea to mention ex-partners, particularly by name. It makes your date feel inadequate.

▶ Tell him your entire past history. Especially your relationship past history. He'll feel overwhelmed, and it'll probably bring up painful feelings for you so you feel awkward. Keep it light.

▶ Moan about your job, your life, your family and especially your exes. Now is the time to accentuate the positive.

And never, ever use the phrase: *I'm no good with men.*

This phrase – and others like it – is entirely banned from your vocabulary around anyone you find attractive. Running yourself down won't make you feel good, it won't make him feel good about you, and it will turn out to be one of those self-fulfilling prophecies.

Negotiating a Second Date (If You Want To)

Do:

▶ Go for it! If you've had a wonderful time and your gut instinct tells you he has too, spare yourself the stress of obsessing afterwards about whether or not he liked you and grasp the nettle. Try saying 'I had a really nice time.' If he doesn't take the hint, add: 'Shall we see one

another again?' or 'Would you like to see me again?'
(like it's a big privilege, not like you're desperate). If
he's vague, then you know it hasn't gone as well as
you think. But at least you know. And if he says yes,
you'll feel wonderful.

Don't:

▶   Say in a scary, needy, graspy way, 'Are you free
    tomorrow?'
▶   Play it too cool if you really like him. Chances are he'll
    take your ice queen act as rejection and disappear
    quicker than an ice pixie.

The Aftermath

Do:

▶   Give him a second chance, even if things didn't go so
    well. The stress, nerves and expectations of a first date
    can make people do some peculiar things.
    Nervousness can make men talk all the time, the
    desire to impress can make some men appear
    arrogant and boastful. Unless he's a complete dork,
    men, like cars and houses, benefit from a second
    viewing.
▶   Use your gut instincts (see page 129) to decide which
    way to go on accepting another date with him or not.

Don't:

▶   Go into a hole if it went badly. It is not the end of the
    world. Even if you liked him and it evidently wasn't
    reciprocated, at least you've found out now, not 10

years down the track. Only a few hours of your precious time have been wasted.

▶ Judge him according to what your friends/parents/ children would think of him. It's *you* who's going to be seeing him in his socks.

▶ Start choosing your bridesmaids or planning your children's schools. Keep expectations down to a minimum. These are very early days. All the women I've talked to about this have had the experience of a perfect first date where the date never called again.

NB If you want to know even more about dating with confidence, read my book Single and Loving It *(Thorsons).*

18

Sexual Self-confidence

When I started having sex, my sexual confidence was zero. I didn't have a clue. The first boy I slept with obviously didn't have a clue either and he used to pull my vulva hard. It was incredibly painful. But I didn't say anything in case that was what you were supposed to do and I was supposed to like it, and I didn't want to look an idiot. The next person I slept with didn't do that, thank goodness, but he did used to do it eight times a night and wore me out. Again, I didn't like to say, 'Give over.' Then I was in a longer relationship, where I was really loved, and he used to ask me what I liked and didn't like, and gradually it dawned on me that it was OK to like some things and not others. That everyone was different. That relationship taught me a lot and I've allowed myself to say 'No thank you' to some things and 'Could you please?' about others ever since.

Lisa, 30, on learning painfully

This might sound loopy, but I had a period between two long relationships where I had several one-night stands. I knew they would be one-nighters or short flings and I found this strangely liberating. I could do just what I liked with these men. I could try things I'd never tried before. I could try out different personalities in bed, sometimes being far more outrageous than I'd ever be with a proper boyfriend. I think it was because there was no 'Oh, what if he won't like me in the morning?' or 'If I ask to go doggie style he might not respect me.' But the men were always fine about it. We had some lovely nights. And it actually helped me to be much freer and more confident in sexual relationships afterwards.

Caroline, 34, on the unexpected joys of one-night stands

If you keep the light off when you're undressing or making love. If you snatch a towel or dressing gown around yourself when you get up to go to the toilet (so he won't see 'bits' wobbling around). If you never orgasm. If you are putting up with an unsatisfactory sojourn between the sheets, meanwhile fantasizing about George Clooney/Brad Pitt/Beppe out of *EastEnders*. If you are avoiding sex altogether because the whole idea is too scary to contemplate. All these are symptoms of lack of sexual confidence.

Sometimes sex is magical between two people. He possesses an invisible map to your love spot and gets there every time. But these are sometimes. It's far more common for there to be *something* that's not right. He strokes you too hard so it hurts, or too soft so it tickles. You do your best back but it doesn't seem to elicit the usual overwhelming enthusiasm. You two just seem to have different sexual rhythms. Worst scenario, he rolls over and falls asleep while you're still high and horny.

In a committed relationship when you know you're going to be getting naked on a regular basis with this person for the foreseeable, you want to get it right. To use a culinary analogy, you don't want to be offered mutton every night when actually you're a vegetarian. But how to say that without dousing his libido and shattering that oh-so-delicate ego?

What Is the *Confident* Thing to Do?

As with everything, the confident thing to do is to *do something*.

It takes confidence to ask for what we want. It takes confidence to let your lover see you in nothing but Chanel No 5. It takes confidence to carefully tell him what works, what doesn't. It takes confidence to suggest *that thing* you fantasize about but have never actually tried. It takes confidence to open up and be vulnerable. And, given our sexual self lies at the very vulnerable heart of our vulnerable self, sexuality can often be our tenderest spot of all.

Just as there are consequences to any lack of self-confidence, there are sad consequences to lacking the courage to speak up around sex. You don't have as enjoyable and fulfilling a sex life as you could. You 'put up' with second best. You may even go off sex altogether and threaten an otherwise good relationship. Plus, you stay stuck. Staying stuck is No Good Thing and only makes you miserable.

If the prospect of sextalk gives you the heebie-jeebies, you are not alone. A straw poll of my female friends revealed they all feel similarly and instinctively that talking to your man about your own sex life is the conversational equivalent of walking on eggs. Mary, 29, is representative: 'The irony is I find it very easy to talk to everyone else about sex, except the person I'm sleeping with. It's pathetic. I can say something very revealing to a total female stranger, or even a man I'm not attracted to, but it's a much slower process with a partner. Right now I've been seeing someone four months and I've started to sneak little things in. I made a little remark the other night and he responded favourably and I think that's a huge move forward, a gateway to getting the sex life I crave with him.'

Esquire magazine surveyed 800 British men, asking them about their sex lives and their sexual attitudes. When it came to talking in bed, several men reported that when they asked their partners, 'What would you like me to do?' invariably the answer would be: 'Whatever you like.'

This is *not* a confident reply!

Any woman who says 'Whatever you like' is metaphorically plunging a hand blindfold into the sexual pix 'n' mix – you never know what you'll come up with. And not only do you risk not liking what you get, it's also not fair on him to have to second guess – then get the blame if he gets it wrong.

Traditionally, it's true, women have hit up against ancient belief structures about how we should be in bed. But this is the 21st century. Those ideas are as outdated as Bros and non-designer kettles. In the *Esquire* survey, 74 per cent of men reckoned their own and their partner's sexual satisfaction were equally important. Of the 26 per cent left, 23 per cent believed that their partner's satisfaction was *more* important than theirs. Only 3 per cent thought their own satisfaction was paramount.

So, unless you're unlucky enough to be sleeping with one of those selfish 3 per cent (in which case, *why?*), the only person stopping you walking round with a grin as wide as Watford is you. So do something about it.

Yes, it may well be scary, but you have plenty of strategies for dealing with the fear. And plenty of women before you have found that, unlike Oliver Twist, asking for more leaves you full and satisfied.

It helps to speak up about sex early on. In the *Esquire* survey, some men pointed out that if you don't share sexual preferences at the beginning of a relationship, communication could become more difficult as time went on. One 30-year-old single man said, 'I can see it's possible that if in the opening year or two you've never really found out what the other person likes, it must become more and more impossible to say ... and you get to the point where it's – "He's always done that and I've never liked it.'"

When It's a New Relationship

Communicating your fears is a terrific intimacy-builder. Rowena, 36, started a new relationship recently, but felt terribly insecure about her new partner seeing her naked because of a Caesarian scar. Using the techniques in this book, remembering to breathe, she found the courage to share her fears, and he replied: 'I love it, it's a part of your history, a part of you.' Now she says: 'If I hadn't mentioned it, I would never have heard that. I felt a rush of tenderness, closeness and a barrier between us melted. That would never have happened if I hadn't had the courage to mention my fears. It also helped me accept that scar. Instead of seeing it as a bad thing, I now see it as a part of my history.'

So Why Don't Woman Speak Up about Sex?

Again: fear. Usually irrational.

We expect – *dread* – bad news. We dread him getting uppity or upset. We dread hearing something we don't want to hear. Like, 'Yes, your bum really *does* look big in that bed.' But in reality, once you get up the courage to talk about your sex life, nine times out of ten it brings you closer. Plus you might find out that, yes, you're brilliant in bed, and all your silly fears can fly out the window. Even if you do hear something less-than-perfect, you then have the option of doing something about it. Of course you run the risk that you will hear something hurtful. But if you do – it's all information. Do you really want to stay with someone who will say hurtful things about your body or how you are sexually?

☆ Star Tip
Do speak up!

You can't lose by speaking out, because even if you hear something bad, it's all grist to the intimacy mill. It tells you more about whom you're sleeping with. And helps you make choices as to whether you sleep with him again in future.

Like Jane, who said, 'I got pregnant and, from about five months onward, Greg seemed to lose enthusiasm when we were making love. He seemed quite distant. I finally got up the courage to ask him what was wrong. I was afraid that it was because I was getting bigger and he didn't fancy me any more. But he said he was actually stressed about becoming a father and that, for him, stress usually affected him sexually. I thought about it and remembered that, once before when he'd been very busy at work, he'd gone distant sexually too. Seemed not to really be there when we were making love. But he said he was glad I brought it up because it caused him to face the issue, and we talked a lot about it and by the time I was eight months' gone we were back on track and at it like rabbits.'

Another thing which holds us back is a lack of self-trust: 'I could never tell him that' – partly because you fear you'd hurt him, partly because you fear you'd make a lash-up of it and say the wrong thing.

But you have tools in your confidence tool kit now. You can coach yourself to talk about sex.

☆ **Star Tip**

> US psychotherapist Stanley Keleman says, 'Loving someone is the willingness to educate them as to who you are.'

That means in bed and out of it. Where's the joy in only being loved for part of yourself?

Steps to Sexual Self-confidence

1. Knowing What You Like

Sex therapists say you can't expect to enjoy a fulfilling sexual relationship with anyone else if you haven't first had one with yourself. *You* need to know what you like. In order to educate a partner about what you like in bed, you have to know your own body's secret sexual pleasures – what turns you on, what you like, what you don't like, what induces bliss, what hits the bullseye and what misses the mark.

In my first book, *Single and Loving It*, I quoted the story of Leah, who discovered the joys of a sexual relationship with yourself at 33 when she split with a long-term boyfriend. She said 'I sent off for a big brown package full of dildos I spotted in a magazine and had the most fantastic fun with my own body.' She said all the cheap Hong Kong dildos fell to pieces the minute she used them, 'but that was part of the fun. And it didn't feel dirty or seedy, it felt like a celebration.' When they'd all bust she went and bought herself a proper vibrator for keeps. She said 'Now I really like sex with my boyfriend and I like sex with myself and they're two different things.' But doing the one helps the other.

2. Liking Your Body

I've mentioned it before; here it is again: you only have one body, so you might as well love it. Clichés become clichés because they always contain an element of truth, and this one is spot on.

Unless you marry a plastic surgeon you really are going to live your life with those legs, those hips, those eyes. And it would be tragic to be still fixating over them 20 years from now.

Psychologist Dr Judith Rodin, author of *Body Traps*, points out how women tend to evaluate their looks according to other women. She says 'Women caught by the competition trap agree with a statement such as: "I'm likely to evaluate how good I look by comparing myself to others." If this is true for you, is it also the case that when you compare your looks to other women's, your relative ranking affects how you feel about yourself?'

All this competition and evaluation erodes confidence. There may be other women with better legs than you, but what are *your* strong points?

Women tend to want to be slim for other women, not for men. Most men love wobbly bits. And if you're in a sexual relationship, he's fancied you enough to go to bed with you, so why are you still trying to hide your cellulite?

Check it out with him. Ask him.

One thing that helps is to do all you can to have the best body you can have. Fitness helps you feel good about yourself. (This does not, however, mean punishing yourself at the gym to achieve some impossible body shape or level of fitness.)

We all know women who are no great stunners but who are happy with their looks. The confidence which oozes off them is what has men gaggling around them at parties. Not their 22-inch waist.

3. Giving Yourself Permission to Ask for What You Want

Don't blurt in the middle of the checkout queue: 'I wish you'd keep going longer.' There are ways of doing this.

One way is, during sex, to move his hand and put it where you'd like it and say, 'Ooh, try it like this … oooh, yes' and lather on plenty of encouragement. And maybe mention it afterwards as being particularly satisfying, as in 'I liked you doing blah blah, that was lovely.' This gentle art of encouragement helps both of you. Appreciation works wonders. Similarly, if he starts doing something you don't like, move his hand away. If he settles in to doing it that old way yet again, be proactive and say: 'Let's try it with me on top' or whatever. Surprise is sexy.

Remember to talk about the behaviour, not the person. Not 'You're a lousy lover, you're inconsiderate, you're so passive.' Say, 'I like it when you move, I'd like you more often to do X.'

If sex is difficult to talk about, it is better to discuss it out of bed. If the issue is deep and painful for you, choose your time and place very carefully, and do tell him it's difficult and painful. If it's just a slight readjustment you're asking for, some experts recommend talking over dinner in a reasonably lighthearted way, when you can also talk about other things you enjoy. That way it's done in a context of appreciating or celebrating sensuality.

Try using books. You can quite neutrally point to a new position and say 'What do you think of that?'

4. It Works Both Ways

Ask him what he likes, whether what you're doing to him feels good. The reply may make you feel like a sex siren.

Don't:

▶ Tell him how it was with other lovers.
▶ Put him down – men's sexual self-confidence is a very fragile thing too.
▶ Talk about what you want to have more or better of in sex when you feel angry, stressed, unattractive, insecure or any one of those things.
▶ Talk in the negative. Say what you want more of, better, different. As far as possible try to minimize a negative. Make your talk aspirational, as in 'This is how we could do this better' rather than 'Here's how you're wrong.'

Tips for Any Kind of Relationship Change

▶ Don't put it off hoping the problem will magically go away. It won't.
▶ Do pick your time to talk – not when the other person is drunk, driving the car, stressed or in a bad mood.
▶ Do listen to what the other has to say.
▶ Try and reach a compromise or an agreement. At all costs, try and have the matter *resolved*. Renowned US marital researcher and therapist John Gottman

believes it is the inability to resolve conflict that does for relationships.

▶ Having said that, you don't have to resolve everything there and then. If things get heated and tiring, you can take time out to calm down.

Exercise

Ponder these questions:

How satisfied am I (marks out of 10, with 10 representing 'very satisfied' and 0 representing 'not satisfied at all') with my sex life? _____

Where does the responsibility for this lie? (i.e. with me or with my partner)_____

What are the payoffs for me putting up with this?
Negative _____ Positive _____

What do I want to do about it? (e.g. Say something to them? See my GP? Try something different?) _____

What am I going to do in the next week/month to tackle this issue? _____

How will I support myself in tackling this? (Breathing and clear communication, discussing it first with a supportive friend, phoning a friend before and after, etc.) _____

What encouraging statements can I make to support myself in doing this? _____

When am I going to tackle this? (e.g. by the end of next week, next month) _____

How committed (marks out of 10, with 10 representing very committed) am I to tackling this? _____

What treat will I give myself afterwards? _____

19

Confidence at Work

It's a bit chicken-and-egg but I would say I am a confident person in a way that I never used to be, even though I was a great big tiger of a boss before. That's because I now know who I am and believe in who and what I am. And when I say something it's coming from my truth. I think to be confident you have to speak your truth. Before I was always thinking people were criticizing me and judging me and so I would tailor myself to what I thought they wanted to hear. I even dressed the way I imagined I ought to dress and I never felt comfortable.

Then I did an evening class in life drawing, followed by an arts foundation course. Doing art allowed me somehow to be who I am. Finding the confidence to show my art to people, to draw in front of people and have them see the results had the effect of stopping me believing people are judging me all the time. I don't feel people are judging me anymore. I can go in and be me and I like me. The other day I went to a business meeting dressed as myself for first time in 35 years and it felt really good. I know it sounds like such a little thing but it felt hugely significant. And it's such a relief.

Lizzie, 35, former magazine editor who now runs creativity workshops, confidently

Remember that pit at the centre of the Colosseum where Russell Crowe in *Gladiator* had to fight everything that was thrown at him? The workplace can feel like that sometimes. It's an arena where all our insecurities, all our fears of failure, all the places where we doubt ourselves come to the fore. Partly because so much is at stake: our career, our livelihood, our future. Am I doing it right? Am I doing OK? Am I about to make an almighty cock-up? Have I *just made* an almighty cock-up? These are as common in the workplace as beige chipboard and nasty coffee.

Relationships at work can be like family relationships. We can get into the same unhelpful grooves with work colleagues and bosses as we do with lovers and siblings.

Unlike family relationships, there are places you can go. If you're being bullied or sexually harassed there are legal recourses. If you're being criticized or undervalued there are other companies or organizations you can go to. If you feel you don't fit in there are other jobs, other careers to go to where you might feel more at home.

All of your shiny new confidence skills will be tested in the workplace. It requires confidence to get a job; it requires confidence to keep one. You need to feel confident to ask for a rise, a promotion, deal with a difficult colleague, to manage people and be managed, leave alone getting the actual task done, whatever it might be. Even leaving requires courage.

Confident Behaviours at Work

Do remember about how knowledge gives you confidence. Arm yourself with as much knowledge as you can about your job. This involves things like making sure you have a job description (so you know what you're supposed to be doing!), making sure you get proper briefings when you get given projects, signing up for any training available, reading up on your subject.

Similarly, know the goals and success criteria for your company/organization and your own personal job. It's hard to know if you're doing a good job if you're not exactly sure what a 'good job' would look like. (And make sure those goals are SMART – see page 111.)

Communicate. Let people around you know what you're doing. And part of good communication is speaking up for yourself and putting yourself forward. Research carried out at IBM revealed that success at work is 10 per cent to do with talent and ability, 30 per cent image and 60 per cent exposure – what you are *seen* to be doing.

All the techniques of confident communication which start on page 81, and those for confident decision-making (page 131) are especially effective in the workplace.

Perhaps getting yourself a mentor would help – someone who knows the ropes and is willing to advise and share their experience with you.

Confidence with Your Boss

A difficult relationship at the best of times. One important tip is to avoid the temptation to slip into child mode (see page 87). The most common complaint from the bosses I train is that they manage a bunch of children. It's common, and all too easy to slip into child with people we perceive as authority figures, but it does us no favours.

Asking too many questions which interrupt those above you is also no way to climb the ladder of success. Bosses like it when you come up with your own solutions. Let him/her know what you're doing, by all means, but do it without having to interrupt constantly. Along the same lines, don't always agree with your boss. Bosses respect people with their own minds.

Appraisals are useful and can build confidence – even if they sometimes pinpoint things we're not getting quite right. Insist on regular appraisals so you know what you're meant to be doing and how you're getting on.

Remember, your boss is a person, too. Work out what motivates them – don't assume everyone is motivated by the same things. It might be status, money, the bottom line. So, do you present your project idea by emphasizing how it'll make them look good, make money, or save money? What's the best way to handle them? How do others do it? If there's a supportive colleague you can ask for feedback about what you do that could be improved and how they handle the boss, then get asking.

Dealing with authority figures is one of the greatest fears of people with social anxiety. If you're doing this, imagine them in their socks, or on the toilet. Get them off that pedestal and into the real world. They're just another human with a job to do. And don't ever let them make you the designated dogsbody – even if you have a dogsbody job. Saying no when you're overloaded is better for everyone. It's better for your stress levels, and your boss will only be furious if you say yes, then can't get it done. See page 102 for tips on saying no.

And If You're the Boss …

Don't fall over backwards trying to make everyone like you all the time. It'll never happen. No one likes conflict, but as a boss you can't possibly avoid it. Nip problems in the bud because, believe me, for every problem that magically went away on its own there are a hundred which got worse with time. Don't beat about the bush if you have to talk to someone about something you don't like. Use the complaint and recommendation structure on page 98. If they have an attitude problem, tell them they have an attitude problem. Remember to tell them how their behaviour affects you and the team – and their likely future career. Keep reminding them of their effect on the *team*. If they fire back, don't be defensive or ask for justification: 'Oh really, what makes you say that?'

Remember the faulty beliefs which increase stress on page 29? You may have some of your own which you create for being a boss, like 'I must have the right answer every time' or 'I have to be aware of everything that's going on with everyone all the time.' You don't.

Do delegate. Bosses who never delegate eventually go pop. Delegating tasks is also one of the most motivating things you can do for those below you, believe it or not. They relish things like responsibility, the chance the impress you, interesting work. Think, 'What's in it for them?' Try and keep focused on the positive aspects – the outcome – rather than the negative aspects – the problem. When children are doing something you don't like, it helps to distract them by offering something you would like them to do. It works with adults too.

Job Interviews

The primary thing to remember about interviewing is: Take your time. The same is true of an appraisal or any conversation where you need to sound confident. Don't rush. Often our desire to please gets us chattering when we'd do ourselves more of a favour to s-l-o-w-d-o-w-n. It's OK to say 'I don't know,' or 'I need a minute to think about that.' In fact, it's more confident than gabbling rubbish. Confidence is about being yourself, not trying to shape yourself into some ideal person who isn't you. Even saying 'I'm a little nervous' is fine. Remember, psychologists say that all the anecdotal evidence shows that expressing awkward feelings always tends to help them go away.

Smile. Even smiling nervously is better than not smiling at all. Remember shy people are often perceived as offish or aloof, just because they're too scared to crack a grin. The same thing goes for making eye contact. Practising at home will help. Use your confidence buddy who knows how you feel and is willing to help you. Role-play an interview situation with them and practise all the things you may want to project, and say. Get them to give you feedback on your body language, how you sound, how you come across. Remember to breathe and feel your feet on the floor.

Do your research. On *Cosmo* I've been appalled by people who wanted a job but hadn't bothered to read the magazine. Familiarize yourself with the company/organization/department in question. That way you can emphasize what *you* can offer them, which is always impressive.

How to Keep It When the Going Gets Tough

When my partner took three months off after taking voluntary redundancy, his first interviewer asked: 'Aren't you worried you'll never work again?' He wasn't, actually, but there's nothing like being presented with this in a job interview to make you start thinking you should be.

Some dastardly things happen when you're looking for a job. The confidence of a Richard Branson would be tested if he had to face 20 or so 'we'll call yous'. Rejection is corrosive to your self-esteem, never mind your confidence. But sometimes you have to face rejection to achieve acceptance. Margaret Mitchell, author of *Gone with the Wind*, was rejected by 38 different publishers before she got a taker for what became one of the biggest-selling books of all time.

► Exercise your anger away. Not only does exercise help work off stress and anger, it also releases feelgood chemicals – endorphins – into your system which will help you feel good about yourself.

► Do something every day towards your dream job. A writer I know started out as a secretary but did something every day. One day she rented a cottage to write in. Now she's a blockbustering novelist.

► Let your support buddy know when you're having a bad day. Let them talk you into a positive mood. Trying to cope all on your own only makes it harder.

► If you find yourself becoming depressed, for God's sake go to the doctor or see a therapist. Depression only creates more depression, and employers can see it oozing out of you.

► Don't take it personally. Novelist Stephen King said, as a young man, he used to spike all his rejection letters on a nail until the nail proved too short for all of them and he had to buy a long spike to put them on. Now he's Stephen King.

► Remind yourself you're mentally toughening yourself with every day that passes. Tell yourself everything that happens, even rejection, is making you stronger. As the philosopher Nietzsche said, 'Whatever doesn't kill me, makes me stronger.'

Exercise

Ponder these questions:

What are my goals at work for the next year? _____
_____

How happy am I with work (marks out of 10, with 10 representing 'very happy' and 0 representing 'not happy at all') at the moment?
_____

What are the payoffs for me putting up with this?
Negative _____ Positive _____

What do I want to do about it? (e.g. Say something to my boss? Ask for more money? Get a different job?) _____
_____

What am I going to do in the next week/month to tackle this issue? _____
_____

How will I support myself in tackling this? (Breathing and clear communication, discussing it first with a supportive friend, phoning a friend before and after, etc.) _____
_____

What encouraging statements can I make to support myself in doing this? _____
_____

When am I going to tackle this? (e.g. by the end of next week, next month) _____
_____

How committed (marks out of 10, with 10 representing very committed) am I to tackling this? _____
_____

What treat will I give myself afterwards? _____
_____

20

Other Confidence-sapping
Occasions

Your Wedding Day

I had been having various difficulties with my husband-to-be and his family before our wedding and I was getting fed up with it. then came the final straw. His mother had got married herself for the second time about six months before our wedding. She asked (at least she asked, I suppose) if it was OK if she wore her wedding outfit to my wedding. Now, I'd been to her wedding and I knew that her wedding outfit had been a big white dress with a big white hat and a veil. She was going to look like the bride! If I'd let it ride I would have worried right up to the moment of walking down the aisle whether she looked more like a bride than me, and I didn't want to put myself through that.

So I took a deep breath and I said no. I put my foot down. I made my partner ring her and tell her it wasn't on. If he'd not agreed to do it I would have done it myself. I was adamant, and I'd never been so clear about anything in my life. And that helped me. I realized that, yes, there were areas where she tried it on, and saying no in this case made it easier in others.
Amanda, 25

If you can't be confident about what you want on *this* day, when can you be? It's an excellent time to practise, to put new behaviours in place, and given getting married is seen as a rite of passage you can take advantage of it to make it a confidence watershed.

Bear in mind people's emotional reactivity is even higher around the time of big family occasions like weddings and anniversaries than they normally are. Their expectations may be higher too. If your mother has always told you what to do, she's likely to do it even more so, have more opinions, now.

This, of all days, is your day. So have what you want. If you want 20 bridesmaids and a tiara like Catharine Zeta Jones', then (finances willing) *have* 20 bridesmaids and said tiara. Don't let anyone sway you from what you want.

It's good to get your new partner on your side. But if you need more confidence in your dealings with *them*, this a good time to put your foot down there too. You don't want to start your new life together on an unconfident foot! You can use this day to set you up for a confident future.

Whatever you do, do have a wonderful time.

☆ Star Tips

▶ On the day: remember to breathe, feel your feet just before and as you walk up the aisle or into the registry office.

▶ Have the confidence to say no to too much to drink – you don't want the best day of your life to go by in a blur!

▶ Find some time in the day to yourself, to gather your thoughts, to savour the moment.

Public Speaking

More than snakes, heights, disease, financial problems or even death, what most people fear most is public speaking. It might be a speech at a wedding, it might be a work presentation, it might be delivering a sermon – whatever the public arena might be it terrifies people – yes – even more than spiders.

Why? The two most common fears are:

1   I might mess up and make a fool of myself.

2   I'm putting myself up there to be judged and they might judge me harshly.

Remember: 90 per cent of what we fear never happens.

Do your preparation thoroughly. Some people advise 10 minutes preparation for every one minute of presenting. Remember how knowing your stuff enables you to feel confident. Practise before-hand. Preferably in front of other people to get feedback, but also in front of a mirror on your own. Practise it for timing. Think about the core purpose of your speech. Don't worry about messing up. If you lose your place, or get something wrong, people usually love you for it. I was at a wedding recently where someone pointed out: 'It's boring if nothing goes wrong with the speeches. Cock-ups make for entertainment.' Remember your right to make a mistake.

On the day, breathe and feel your feet on the floor. Check any visual aids beforehand. You don't want to find the slides are in the wrong order when you're actually doing the speech. Walk *slowly* up the podium, or wherever you're doing it. Speak slowly. Breathe throughout. Look at your audience. Make eye contact with some-one. This helps both you and them.

Keep it short and sweet. You don't want to run on or bore people; or run out of time and leave your most important points (or best jokes) out. Once again, *be yourself*. Unless you've trained in acting, don't try to be someone else. When I did presentation training, the trainers advised letting your own personality shine through. That way, people warm to you. Speak as you'd speak. Don't use long, pompous or unfamiliar words. Keep it simple. Keep thinking about your purpose. Are you getting it across?

Getting Your Doctor to Listen

This is a tricky one for many women. Even if your doctor is a woman, you may find yourself quaking at the very idea of stand-ing up for yourself in the surgery. But stay calm (keep breathing). Don't whinge or play victim. It'll make him/her unsympathetic to your cause.

Nor should you beat around the bush. Doctors usually only allo-cate 10 minutes per patient. Once you've stated what's wrong, keep stating it and what you'd like. Boil it down to a core phrase. Use broken record if necessary. Don't take no (or never mind) for an answer.

If all else fails, ask for – and get – a second opinion. Make a fuss. It's your health and it's *important*.

Complaining in a Shop or Restaurant

Another bugbear, but with all your confidence techniques you will be able to handle it this time. Take a deep breath and just do it.

Yes, there might be a moment of discomfort. Yes, the other person might not like what you're saying. If it's a restaurant, your fellow diners might feel embarrassed. But no one will judge you harshly for it. If it's not right, it's not right. And you're paying for it.

Remember to have a core phrase and stick to it. Include in your statement telling them what you want: 'This meat is underdone and I'd like it well done, as I asked for'; or 'This jumper shrank after one wash and I want my money back/a refund/a replacement.' Persist. If you don't hear what you want to hear first time, don't cave in. Stick to your guns. Use broken record and keep repeating your core phrase until you get a result. If you don't get a result, go above their head. Ask to see the manager. Then repeat the core phrase and broken record with him/her. All the time, try and stay calm. Keep breathing. Don't resort to insults unless they do.

If all else fails, call Anne Robinson!

Summary of Part Three

You now know everything you need to know in order to coach yourself to be that confident person you always dreamed of. And there *is* a confident person inside you; armed with all the tools you have now, that person can blossom.

Quietly and gently at first, taking baby steps. But then getting more and more confident as you practise until you'll be able to muster up all the courage to look your confident role model in the eye and say, 'Yes, I can do it too.' I promise you the feeling will be so wonderful, the changes that happen in your life as a result so positive, you will never slip back into 'I can't do it' again. Once you know you *can*, the world's out there for the courageous taking.

My one wish for you is that you find yourself the initial courage to really try, to genuinely practise these tools. Because, as I've said over and over, they work. Just do it and see the difference.

Good luck!